FOCUS ON HISPANIC AMERICANS

Author:
Angela Allen

Illustrators:
Sue Fullam
Agi Palinay

Cover Artist:
Kathy Bruce

Editor:
Stephanie Avera

Editor-in-Chief:
Sharon Coan, M.S. Ed.

Editorial Project Manager:
Karen J. Goldfluss, M.S. Ed.

Art Director:
Elayne Roberts

Product Manager:
Phil Garcia

Imaging:
Hillary Merriman

Publishers:
Rachelle Cracchiolo, M.S. Ed.
Mary Dupuy Smith, M.S. Ed.

Teacher Created Materials, Inc.
P.O. Box 1040
Huntington Beach, CA 92647
©1995 Teacher Created Materials, Inc.
Made in U.S.A.
ISBN-1-55734-498-1

Table of Contents

Introduction

If one were to ask a student, or an adult for that matter, to name some famous Hispanic Americans, he or she would probably count no higher than the five fingers on one hand. United States Census Bureau data predicts that after the year 2000, not only will Hispanics become the largest ethnic group in the United States, but there will be no single ethnic majority. Clearly, the United States is increasingly becoming more linguistically and culturally diverse. Students need to be educated and must be encouraged to recognize the many contributions to our country made by all Americans.

The purpose of *Focus on Hispanic Americans* is to broaden teachers' and students' knowledge of the contributions made by notable contemporary Hispanic Americans. This book has been divided into five sections for easy reference: Education and

Scholarship, Fine Arts, Science and Medicine, Sports, and Civic Leadership. Within each section are biographical sketches of selected Hispanic Americans. On the same page with each biography is a picture or graphic representation of the Hispanic American. Next is a page of suggested activities which you can include in your lesson plans.

Following the activities is a bibliography of related reading material (trade books, fiction, and periodicals). A student's activity page is also supplied for each Hispanic American. The student page reinforces an aspect of the person's life or accomplishments.

Focus on Hispanic Americans will enable you to present some fascinating and motivational information to students. The inspiring stories of these men and women will encourage teachers and students to consider multiple perspectives when studying any field.

Using the Pages

How you use this book depends on a number of factors, including school district curriculum guidelines, learning levels of the students, your teaching style and goals, how well a topic blends with a particular theme, or your own interest in a particular area. The following descriptions of the book's features are intended to help you get the most from each page.

Sections

Focus on Hispanic Americans begins with general information about Hispanic culture and the origins of Hispanic Americans. These pages introduce customs, language, and foods.

The remainder of the book consists of brief biographical sketches of notable contemporary Hispanics in five broad fields: Education and Scholarship, Fine Arts, Science and Medicine, Sports, and Civic Leadership. Many of the people featured have made contributions in more than one area, but were placed in a certain category for purposes of this book. Following the biographies in each section there are related activities.

Biographies

As an introduction to interest students in biographies, make one copy of each biography. Decorate a loose leaf binder cover to make a book of biographies, and put a copy of each biography in the binder. Leave a blank piece of paper behind each biography page. Encourage students to find additional information on the personalities featured. They can write any facts they learn on the paper behind the biographies. Students can add their own biography pages about other famous Hispanic Americans.

Make a set of biography cards. Copy the picture or name of each Hispanic American, and glue it to an index card. Write the important biographical data about the person on the card. Store all cards in an index file for quick reference.

Themes

While this book can be used as a complete unit of study on Hispanic Americans, you may decide to use the information to integrate Hispanic personalities into other units of study. For example, in a unit of study on space and the space program, one could use the biographies of Franklin Chang-Diaz and Ellen Ochoa, or use the biography of Angela de Hoyos in a unit of poetry and poets.

Extending the Section

Several extension ideas follow each section. Choose those which are best suited to your classroom needs and adapt them to fit your students' abilities and your teaching style. Another option is to allow students to choose their activities. A list of recommended reading provides a selection of related references available to teachers and students. Check your school, public, or university library for other titles. Look for *Books in Print* or *Best Books for Children* (both published by R.R. Bowker) and *Eyeopeners!* by Betty Kobrin (Penguin Books, 1988) in the reference section to help you find more titles.

Student Pages

These pages accommodate a number of learning levels. Decide which of these activities are suitable for your students and feel free to alter the directions if necessary.

A brief bibliography follows the activities. It provides a selection of related references available to teacher and students. Check your school, public, or university library for other titles.

Multicultural Education

The intent of multicultural education is to provide a diversity of perspectives to students and to broaden students' knowledge and experience of the world. A multicultural education enables students to learn about the contributions of all peoples to society as well as provide a vehicle to eliminate bias in the curriculum.

The authors of *The Anti-Bias Curriculum* cite research that indicates that racism and bias are not only harmful to children of color but to all children. Some teachers may argue that they do not need a multicultural curriculum because their schools are comprised of primarily one ethnic group. A White, middle-class school can benefit from a multicultural curriculum as much as a Spanish bilingual school or as much as a racially diverse inner-city school. Multicultural education does more than make students feel good about themselves and is concerned with the feelings of all children, not just those of minority students. A multicultural education prepares all students for their futures in a linguistically and culturally diverse nation and world.

Furthermore, a multicultural curriculum contains aspects that, when used effectively, can lead to success for all children. So what is a multicultural curriculum? What does it look like? Many view multicultural education as subject matter integration. For this reason, a math teacher may say that multicultural education does not apply to her. However, content integration is but one part of a complete multicultural curriculum. According to James A. Banks, multicultural education has five components: subject matter integration, the process of knowledge construction, prejudice reduction, a pedagogy of equity, and a school culture and social structure that is empowering. Multicultural education is not something to be added on to existing curriculum; rather, it is an integral part of curriculum.

Many authors such as Banks, Ogbu, Giroux, Friere, and Darder, to name a few, have written extensively on the theories of critical pedagogy and effective educational approaches for bicultural education. The California Department of Education has also developed a system model for school districts planning multicultural education.

The many authors and models do provide guidelines on implementation, but it is up to educators to actively promote and apply multiculturalism to the classroom. All children can develop an awareness and understanding of other cultural groups as well as to accept individual and group differences. We live in a multicultural world in which all people belong to ethnic groups and in which we can find traditions that justify pride.

Multicultural education is an integral part of the curriculum.

Hispanic Americans: Who Are They?

The term *Hispanic American* refers to people or their descendants who originally came from Spanish-speaking countries. The common language is Spanish, but the countries are varied. However, not all Hispanic Americans speak Spanish. In some families the generations born here in the United States speak only English, and the Spanish language has been lost. Hispanics are currently the fastest growing minority group in the United States, and in some states, such as California, they make up the largest minority group.

The three largest Hispanic groups in the United States are Cubans, Puerto Ricans, and Chicanos.

Chicano, a term that was coined during the civil rights era is a proud name for people of Mexican descent living in the United States. Sometimes Hispanics will use the term Latino, which refers to peoples from Latin America (Spanish-speaking countries in North and South America, excluding Puerto Rico, Cuba, and Spain). Most Hispanics in this country can trace their family history to one of the countries listed in the diagram below.

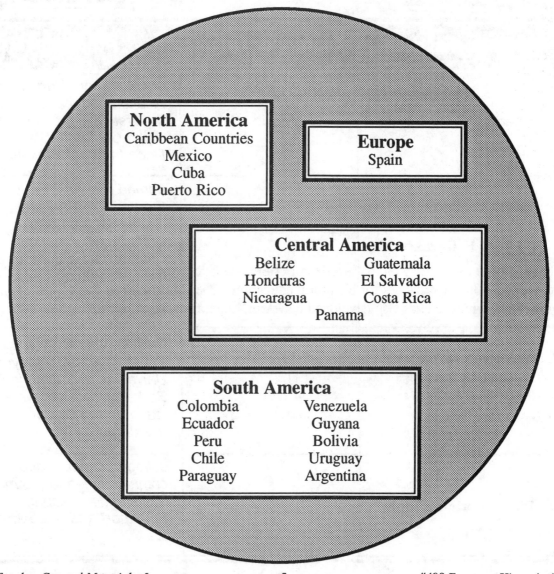

North America
Caribbean Countries
Mexico
Cuba
Puerto Rico

Europe
Spain

Central America
Belize	Guatemala
Honduras	El Salvador
Nicaragua	Costa Rica
Panama	

South America
Colombia	Venezuela
Ecuador	Guyana
Peru	Bolivia
Chile	Uruguay
Paraguay	Argentina

Education and Scholarship

Below is a listing of the Hispanic Americans represented in this section. Following each name is the Hispanic American's country of origin and a brief statement about his or her achievements.

Hispanic American	Country of Origin	Achievements
Armando M. Rodriguez	Mexico	*advocate for bilingual and bicultural education, became the first Chicano consultant to the California State Department of Education*
Dr. Lauro F. Cavazos, Jr.	U. S. A.	*named Hispanic Educator of the Year by the Texas chapter of the League of United Latin American Citizens in 1983, received the Outstanding Leadership Award in Education from President Reagan*
Patricia Zavella	U. S. A.	*received her M. A. and Ph. D. in anthropology at the University of California in Berkeley; teacher, writer, leader in the Chicana movement*
Tessa Martinez Tagle	U. S. A.	*college president and community leader; named "Outstanding Hispanic Educator" and a "Leader of the 80s"*

Armando M. Rodriguez

Bilingual and Bicultural Advocate

Armando M. Rodriguez has had a distinguished career in education and is an advocate for bilingual and bicultural education. He has written numerous articles and made many speeches in support of bilingual education. Evidence of this support can be seen in his active involvement in organizations such as the National Education Task Force de la Raza, National Urban Coalition, and Hispanic Urban Center. He serves on the Board of Trustees for Raza Association of Spanish Surnamed Americans. He is recognized as an educator, administrator, and college president.

Armando M. Rodriguez was born in Mexico but became a naturalized United States citizen. He was born on September 30, 1921, in a small town called Gomez Palacios. He had thirteen brothers and sisters, and when he was ten years old his parents left their home in the state of Durango, Mexico, and emigrated to the United States. Armando Rodriguez grew up and went to public schools in San Diego, California.

In World War II, Armando Rodriguez joined the army and served in the signal corps. He was able to go to college after the war by using the G. I. Bill, which enables soldiers to receive financial assistance for college. He graduated from San Diego State University (then called San Diego State College) in 1949 with his bachelor's degree.

While he was teaching junior high school in San Diego, he continued his studies for a master's degree and received it from San Diego State in 1951. From the junior high school classroom, Rodriguez accepted a job as guidance consultant for San Diego schools. He later became a vice-principal of a junior high school and then principal of a high school. In 1965, the same year he began his principalship, he became the first Chicano consultant to the California State Department of Education.

In 1967 he moved to Washington, D. C., to direct the Office for Spanish Speaking American Affairs. In 1970 at the University of California, Riverside, he was a Regents Lecturer. In 1973 he was selected from more than one hundred applicants to become president of East Los Angeles College. In 1978 President Jimmy Carter appointed Rodriguez to the Equal Opportunity Employment Commission, where he served until the term ended in 1983.

Besides serving in many organizations related to education, Rodriguez has been awarded such honors as the Award for Outstanding Performance from the Department of Health, Education, and Welfare Secretary. He also received an honorary doctoral degree from John F. Kennedy College in Nebraska.

Suggested Activities

Armando M. Rodriguez is an advocate for bilingual and bicultural education. The following suggested activities will help students to explore the issues involved in bilingual and bicultural education as well as some of the problems experienced by bicultural students.

1. **Immigrants.** Read the stories *Coming to America* and/or *Molly's Pilgrim* (see listing below). Imagine that you are one of the immigrants coming to a new country. You will have to leave behind most of your friends and relatives. Who will you miss the most? You can take only what you can carry. What will you take? You will be surrounded by people speaking different languages. How will you communicate?

2. **Storytelling.** Storytelling is an important part of Hispanic culture. Stories are used to preserve traditions and to share values and beliefs. A good storyteller uses emotion, body movements, and lots of expression. However, no two storytellers tell the same story in exactly the same way. Choose a favorite short story and tell (rather than read) the story to your classmates. You can do this as an individual or in a group.

3. **Folktales.** Folktales often have a moral or message at the end. Read the following Hispanic folktale. Think about the message at the end. Can you write a story of your own that would express the same message?

"Los Ratoncitos"
(The Little Mice)

Once there were three little mice who lived with their mother in a hole under the ground. Because they were very young, they had not been outside and wanted to see the world. One day they asked their mother if they could go out for a walk, and she agreed. Suddenly, she heard her ratoncitos crying, "Mama, el gato, the cat!" The mother rushed out and confronted the cat, saying "Bow, wow, bow, wow," and the cat ran away. After counting her babies to make sure they were all safe and accounted for, she told them, "It is always good to know the language of the country you are living in."

Recommended Reading

Molly's Pilgrim by Barbara Cohen (Lothrop, 1983)

New Kids in Town: Oral Histories of Immigrant Teens by Janet Bode (Scholastic Inc., 1991)

Coming to America: The Kid's Book about Immigration by David Fassler & Kimberly Danforth (Waterfront, 1992)

A Family of Fourteen

Armando M. Rodriguez grew up in a house of 13 brothers and sisters. Think about what it would be like to have 13 brothers and sisters and answer the following questions.

1. Name three advantages of having 13 brothers and sisters.

   _____

   _____

   _____

2. Name three disadvantages of having 13 brothers and sisters.

   _____

   _____

   _____

3. Would you want to be in a family of 14 children? Why or why not?

   _____

   _____

   _____

4. From a parent's point of view, what would be the most difficult aspect of having 14 children? What would be the best aspect of having 14 children?

Most Difficult Part	**Best Part**
_____	_____
_____	_____
_____	_____
_____	_____
_____	_____
_____	_____

5. Families seem to be getting smaller; why do you think this is happening? Write your ideas here. Use the back of this paper if necessary.

   _____

   _____

   _____

Dr. Lauro F. Cavazos, Jr.

Author and Educator

Lauro Cavazos' father was working on the King Ranch in Texas when Lauro was born on January 4, 1927. Lauro F. Cavazos, Jr. completed high school and went on to study zoology at Texas Technological University in Lubbock, Texas. He earned his bachelor's and master's degrees in Lubbock. At the young age of twenty-seven Cavazos had completed his Ph. D. in physiology at Iowa State University in 1954.

Dr. Cavazos is respected as a professor, administrator, author, and university president. He has been active in community affairs, and in 1983 he was named Hispanic Educator of the Year by the Texas chapter of the League of United Latin American Citizens.

Dr. Cavazos began his career in education by teaching anatomy at the Medical College of Virginia. He soon advanced from instructor to associate professor. During the ten-year period he taught at Tufts University School of Medicine, he advanced from associate dean to acting dean to dean of the school. In 1980 he was selected as president of Texas Technological University, interestingly, the place in which he began his medical studies.

Over the years, Dr. Cavazos has contributed articles to medical journals as well as authoring articles for texts. He co-authored two dissecting guides for anatomy and physiology courses. He was recognized as a distinguished alumnus from both of the universities he attended, Texas Tech and Iowa State.

As well as being called upon to serve as advisor and consultant to a variety of organizations, including ___ Health Organization, Dr. Cavazos has been the recipient of many awards. In 1984 ___ed Cavazos with the Outstanding Leadership Award in the Field of ___ Distinguished Service Medal from the Uniformed Services

Suggested Activities

1. **Goals.** Dr. Cavazos earned his doctorate degree at the age of twenty-seven, which meant that he had to continually go to school and study very hard. He set a goal for himself and worked to achieve it. Have students set daily and weekly goals for themselves. Design a chart or record to help monitor progress toward the goal or use the chart on page 12.

2. **Setting Your Goals.** When students understand what is important to them they better understand how to make choices and set goals. Fold a piece of paper into eight sections (or use index cards if more space is needed). Ask students to write a subject area (math, science, art, social studies, writing, etc.) in each section and draw a graphic that represents that subject. For example, in the math section, students may draw number equations or symbols and in the reading section, a book. Use a sentence strip or long strip of paper and have students cut apart and glue each piece in order of what is most important to least important to them. Share with classmates their sequences of what is important to them in the school day. Discuss why a certain subject may be more important because of future plans.

3. **Obstacles.** Ask students to think about their wishes and dreams and then to think about what obstacles they may face in achieving their dreams. Ask students to choose the biggest obstacles that would hinder their progress towards their dreams. Have each student write the obstacle on a strip of paper. Place a scented candle in a large glass or casserole dish. Have a classroom ceremony in which students burn their pieces of paper with their obstacles in the flame of the candle. Discuss with students how the candle burning ceremony made them feel and whether if it will help them reach their goals. (Adult supervision and safety precautions are necessary for this activity.)

Recommended Reading _____

Stand and Deliver by Nicholas Edwards. (This was also produced as a movie featuring actor Edward James Olmos). *Stand and Deliver* is a moving story about a teacher who had a dream of success for his students and did not let them give up on their dreams.

My Goal for Today

Name_____ Date _____

Today I will try to _____

_____

_____

Each time you remember, color a star. Each time you forget, color a stop sign.

☆   ☆   ☆   ☆   ☆

☆   ☆   ☆   ☆   ☆

I remembered _____ times.

STOP   STOP   STOP   STOP   STOP

STOP   STOP   STOP   STOP   STOP

I forgot _____ times.

Use your own ideas to design a weekly goals chart. At the end the week, review your progress in achieving your goals. After a few weeks, compare your charts. How did you do?

Patricia Zavella

Educator and Anthropologist

Being the oldest of twelve children, Patricia Zavella helped her mother to care for her large family. She had her love of reading as a retreat from her other responsibilities. Patricia's father was in the air force, so the family moved as her father was transferred from base to base.

When she was in the sixth grade her father left the air force and got a job as an electronics technician in Ontario, California. In her early schooling, Patricia felt that her teachers had low expectations of her because she was Mexican-American. In high school, however, she was challenged and encouraged to continue her education. In 1971 she received her A. A. degree from Chaffey College in Alta Loma, California, and in 1973 she received her B. A. degree in anthropology from Pitzer College in Claremont, California. Zavella went on to complete her M. A. and Ph. D. in anthropology at the University of California in Berkeley.

As a result of her involvement during college in various Hispanic organizations and activities, Zavella began thinking about how Mexicans are treated in the United States. She has a strong commitment to the Chicano movement, which can be seen in her teaching and writing. Her interests in the field of anthropology are work, family structures, and research methods. In particular, she is interested in the role of women in the workplace and the effects women have on their families.

Patricia Zavella, educator and anthropologist, became associate professor in 1989 at the University of California at Santa Cruz, where she lives with her partner and two children. She serves as a consultant to various studies of family structure, and she often contributes articles to journals. She wrote a book in 1987, *Women's Work and Chicano Families: Cannery Workers of the Santa Clara Valley*, that arose from her dissertation research. She was interested in a discrimination suit that had been filed by women cannery workers against the food processing plant where they worked.

Zavella moved to San José and lived in the same community as the workers, conducted interviews, and took notes in an attempt to understand their lives. With her findings she wrote her first book that dealt with the culture of Chicano workers.

Suggested Activities

1. **"Real" Americans.** Patricia Zavella is a strong proponent of Chicanos' rights. Chicanos are second or third generation Mexicans that were born in this country. Some face discrimination as women and as people of Mexican descent even though they are United States citizens. Sometimes it is said that they are not "real" Americans.

   Discuss with your classmates what it means to be American.

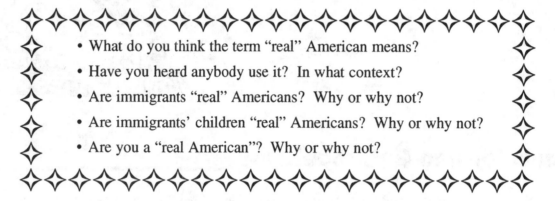

   * What do you think the term "real" American means?
   * Have you heard anybody use it? In what context?
   * Are immigrants "real" Americans? Why or why not?
   * Are immigrants' children "real" Americans? Why or why not?
   * Are you a "real American"? Why or why not?

   If you answered no to any of the questions, what would make someone a "real" American? How could someone become a "real" American?

2. **Reading.** Although Patricia grew up with family responsibilities, she always had a love for reading. Name three books you have read that were written by or were about people of a different religion, language, or culture from yourself. Reading is one of the best ways to learn about others. Look at the recommended readings in this book or ask your librarian for suggestions.

3. **Anthropology.** Patricia Zavella is an anthropologist. Learn more about this science. What is the definition of anthropology? What are some responsibilities of an anthropologist? Patricia Zavella's interests in anthropology are with the family structure. What are some other areas of anthropology? What other areas could be studied that might interest you?

Recommended Reading _____

New Moon: The Magazine for Girls and their Dreams by New Moon Publishers, P.O. Box 3587, Duluth, MN, 55803 (*New Moon* is a bimonthly publication designed to empower and inspire girls to be themselves and to value achievement.)

Why Am I Different? by Norma Simon (A Whitman, 1976)

Extraordinary Hispanic Americans by Susan Sinnott (Childrens, 1991)

Immigration by Patricia Sima, Sharon Coan, Ina Massler Levin, and Karen Goldfluss (Teacher Created Materials, 1993)

Hispanic American Struggle for Equality by Jeffry Jensen (Rourke Corp., 1992)

Multicultural Book Report

Patricia Zavella has said that reading helped her escape from all of the responsibilites that faced her in her young life. Reading has provided comfort and encouragement to people throughout their lives. It allows us to expand our knowledge and understanding of people and places. Reading also gives us hours of entertainment and pleasure.

Choose a book to read that represents a culture with which you would like to become more familiar. After reading the book, complete the book report below and share it with your class.

Title: _____

Author(s): _____

Type of Book: Fiction _____   Nonfiction _____

This book represents the _____ culture.

I feel it is a **good, bad** *(circle one)* representation because_____

_____

On a scale of **1–5,** I would rate this book _____ because _____

_____

_____

My favorite part of the book was_____

_____

_____

_____

I would, would not *(circle one)* recommend this book to others because_____

_____

_____

_____

_____

_____

Tessa Martinez Tagle

Community Leader

Tessa Martinez Tagle was born in San Antonio, Texas, in 1947. Her mother died when Tessa was only two years old, and she was raised by her two grandmothers and an aunt. Her father worked in Mexico for the U. S. Department of Agriculture. When she was a little girl, she often went to visit her father where he worked in the mountains and jungles. She spent time with her father among the Indians and learned to speak one of the Indian dialects. Her grandmothers and father were influential in motivating her to succeed. It was her mother's wish that she would go to college and be successful, and her father promised to make the wish come true.

After being encouraged in high school, Tessa Martinez Tagle pursued journalism in college and received her degree from the University of Texas in Austin in 1969. At that time it was difficult for women to break into journalism, so she began her career by teaching high school in San Antonio and later lecturing in community college. She went into administration at San Antonio College and was named dean of Occupational, Technical, and Continuing Education in 1984.

In the meantime, Tessa Martinez Tagle continued her own education by obtaining her master's degree in education and business from the University of Texas in San Antonio, and she eventually earned a Ph. D. in educational administration from the University of Texas at Austin in 1988.

When she was offered the job as college president of Miami/Dade Community College Medical Center Campus in 1988, Tessa Martinez Tagle was ready to accept the challenge. She has gained respect and won several awards for her dedication as college president and outreach to the community at large.

Tessa Martinez Tagle is a member of several educational organizations and was named "Outstanding Hispanic Educator" and a "Leader of the 80s."

Suggested Activities

1. **Family Trees.** Tessa Martinez Tagle was raised by her two grandmothers and her father. Explain to students that family is very important in Hispanic cultures, and many people not only call their own relatives family but also have "compadres" or godparents who are usually close friends of the parents of the child. Have students complete family trees similar to the one on page 18. Display the trees around the room. Students may also wish to arrange photographs or sketches of their family members around the trees.

2. **Surnames.** Point out to students that in some Hispanic names it seems as if the person has two last names; that is because traditionally Mexicans do have two surnames. For example, for a person whose name is Maria Alvarez Gonzalez, Maria is her first name. Alvarez is the last name of her father, and Gonzalez is the last name of her mother (her mother's maiden name).

   If Maria were to marry a man named Juan Martinez Cordova she could then make her name Maria Alvarez Gonzalez de Martinez. She would add her husband's first surname, but, the husband's name stays the same.

   Most Mexican Americans do not follow the traditional practice, but some Mexican American women are beginning to use their maiden names again. Ask students to write surnames for members of their families. They can use the information from their family trees.

3. **The Mountains.** When Tessa was a little girl, she often went to visit her father where he worked in the mountains of Mexico. Most of Mexico's mountains are volcanoes. Two well-known ones are Popocatepetl, which is Indian for "Smoking Mountain," and Ixtaccihuatl, which means "White Lady." The Aztecs believed these two mountains were gods. The legend is that Popocatepetl was a warrior in love with the Aztec Emperor's beautiful daughter, Ixtaccihuatl. Ixta mistakenly believed Popo had been killed at war, and she died of grief. When Popo returned, he laid her body on the mountain and stood guard over her, holding a burning torch.

   Have students research legends and true stories of Mexico's volcanic mountains. Ask them to complete one of the following activities.

   1. Have students make up their own mountains and write legends about how the mountains came into existence.

   2. An excellent book is *Hill of Fire* (see listing below). This is a true story of the 1943 eruption of Paricutin volcano in Mexico. Ask students to make up a story that would give a different explanation of why El Monstruo (the monster) is there.

Recommended Reading _____

Felita by Nicholasa Mohr (Dial Books, 1979)

Hill of Fire by Thomas P. Lewis (Harper & Row, 1971)

Family Tree

Fill in the following family tree with your family information.

Nombre (name) _____

_____
abuelo
(grandfather)

_____
abuela
(grandmother)

_____
abuelo
(grandfather)

_____
abuela
(grandmother)

_____
tías/tíos
(aunts/uncles)

_____
papá
(father)

_____
mamá
(mother)

_____
tías/tíos
(aunts/uncles)

_____
hermanos
(brothers)

_____
yo (me)

_____
hermanas
(sisters)

Other family members: _____

Primos/primas (cousins) _____

Bisabuelo/bisabuela _____

(great grandfather/great grandmother)

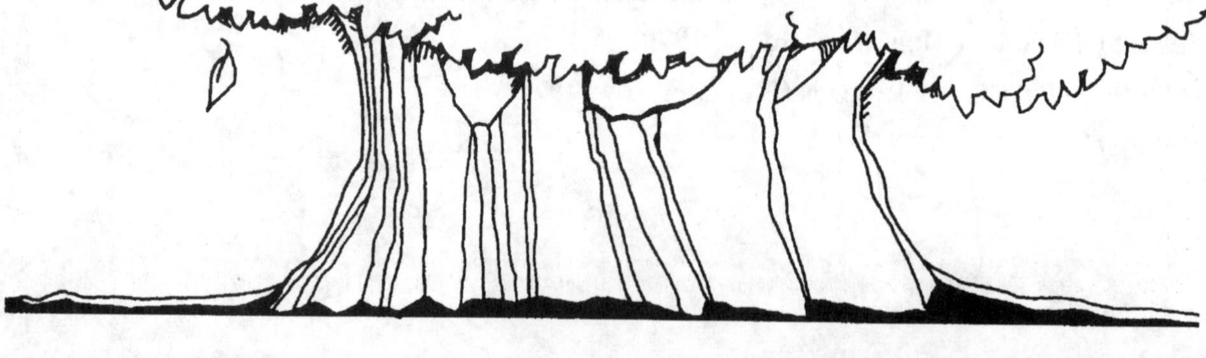

On the Subject of Writing

Many of the Hispanic Americans you have studied in this section have written articles and books during their careers. Whether they wrote essays, college papers, or journal articles, the authors had to constantly write and revise their work in order to improve the quality. This is part of the writing process called *editing*. Try editing your own, or someone else's, writing by using the following standard marks to show where improvements are needed.

Proofreading Marks

Symbol	Meaning	Example
≡	Capitalize.	david gobbled up the grapes.
/	Make lower case.	My mother hugged Me when I came Home.
⊙	Add a period.	The clouds danced in the sky⊙
sp.	Correct spelling mistake.	sp. I laffed at the story.
∽	Reverse words or letters.	How you are?
∧	Add a word.	please Would you pass the pizza?
∧,	Add a comma.	I have two cats two dogs and a goldfish.
ℓ	Delete. (get rid of)	Will you call call me on the phone tonight?

19

American Place Names

Since much of the Western United States once belonged to Mexico, and since Spanish explorers were in North America many years ago, some cities and even states have names borrowed from the Spanish language. Look at the names of places listed below. See whether you can match the Spanish place name with its meaning. Remember that *cognate* words are words that are similar in both languages. Many of the clues will not be difficult. Use a dictionary if needed.

Fill in the spaces at the bottom of the page by writing the places and their meanings.

Place	Meaning
Los Angeles	the passage
Colorado	city of angels
San Francisco	mountain
Montana	tile roof
San Antonio	the crossroads
Las Cruces	Saint Francis
Texas	colored red
Santa Fe	Holy Faith
El Paso	Saint James
San Diego	Saint Anthony

_____ means _____

_____ means _____

_____ means _____

_____ means _____

_____ means _____

_____ means _____

_____ means _____

_____ means _____

_____ means _____

_____ means _____

Challenge: Use a reference book to find other places whose names have been borrowed from the Spanish language. Write the information on the back of this page.

Fine Arts

Below is a listing of Hispanic Americans represented in this section. Following each name is the Hispanic American's country of origin and a brief statement about his or her achievements.

Hispanic American	Country of Origin	Achievements
Linda Ronstadt	U.S.A.	Broadway actress and world famous musician
Joan Baez	U.S.A.	folk singer and political activist
Amado Maurilio Pena	U.S.A.	storyteller and artist in the Southwestern tradition
Luis M. Valdez	U.S.A.	playwright, dramatist, founder of El Teatro Campesino
Carmen Zapata	U.S.A.	actress, dancer, founder of Bilingual Foundation for the Arts
José Antonio Burciaga	U.S.A.	muralist, writer of social commentary
Angela de Hoyos	Mexico	bilingual poet
Gloria and Emilio Estefan	Cuba	world famous Latin musicians and community activists

Linda Ronstadt

Musician and Broadway Actress

As a young girl, Linda Ronstadt used to listen to her father as he sang and played Mexican music. Her father owned a hardware store in Tuscon, Arizona, where she was born in 1946. She loved to sing in harmony with her brothers and sister. Her family spoke Spanish at home, but after going to school she learned and spoke mostly English. At that time, schools were very much against children speaking their native languages, and children were even punished for speaking anything other than English.

At age eighteen Linda Ronstadt dropped out of the University of Arizona and went to Los Angeles with her boyfriend, Bob Kimmel. They formed a group called the Stone Poneys with another musician. They signed a contract with Capitol Records and released a single and two albums. However, the group did not gain in popularity, and the Stone Poneys broke up. Linda decided to fulfill the recording contract with Capitol Records by going solo. She produced several albums, but her first few years as a singer were difficult. She was unaccustomed to the stresses of being a popular singer, living on the road, hectic schedules, and relationships.

In 1973 Ronstadt changed recording companies by moving to Asylum Records, and she asked Peter Asher to be her manager. Some of her hits in the 1970s included "You're No Good," "Blue Bayou," and "Desperado." She released several albums that sold over a million copies. Her singing style began as a mix of country and rock, and she soon became one of the hottest female pop rock singers. The greatness of her voice proved itself over and over again as she diverged from the pop rock style in the 1980s.

Broadway challenged Linda Ronstadt to use the full extent of her vocal capabilities. She appeared in the Broadway play, *The Pirates of Penzance*, in the soprano part of Mabel in 1981.

Again, in 1984 she played the part of Mimi in an off-Broadway production of *La Boheme*. In 1987 as if to come full circle back to her roots, Linda Ronstadt released an album of mariachi songs that her father used to sing, entitled *Canciones de Mi Padre (Songs of My Father)*. In 1991 she starred in *La Pastorela*, a Mexican holiday play, on PBS. She also released another album called *Mas Canciones (More Songs)*, a sequel to *Canciones de Mi Padre*.

Suggested Activities

1. **Mariachi.** Linda Ronstadt's father used to sing mariachi songs. A mariachi band is a strolling orchestra complete with stringed instruments such as the guitar, guitarron (like a large guitar), violin, and viola, along with cornets and trumpets. Traditionally, mariachi musicians are male, but there are many female mariachis today. Listen to a tape of mariachi music. See whether you can identify the different instruments that are being played.

2. **Drums.** Make your own drums with oatmeal boxes or coffee cans with the lids. Cut a piece of paper the height of the drum base and wide enough to be glued around it. Draw or paint a dazzling design and decorate with glitter, strings, beads, or buttons. Use your imagination. Practice playing along with a mariachi song.

3. **The Expression of Music.** You will need a marker and a piece of paper. Listen to a piece of music and allow the marker to flow freely across the page as you listen. The marker should move in a way that expresses how you feel about the music. Keep your eyes open so that you can see what you are doing but remember to feel freedom of movement. Do not draw something, allow the marker to flow. After the music stops, use more markers to color in the spaces of the design that you have made. No white spaces should remain on the page. Mount designs on solid colored construction paper and display. Try this activity with different kinds of music.

4. **Family Traditions.** Although Linda Ronstadt was a rock/pop singer, she did record some albums that reflected her family heritage. Think about family traditions that you have. What are some that you have that you would like to preserve?

Recommended Reading _____

The Skirt by Gary Soto (a story about a girl who borrows her mother's folkloric skirt for a dance performance at school) (Dell, 1994)

Linda Ronstadt: Mexican American Singer, Hispanics of Achievement Series (Chelsea House, 1991)

Songs of Hispanic Americans, edited by Ruth DeCesare (Alfred Publishing, 1991)

Multicultural Portrait of America's Music by David P. Press (Marshall Cavendish, 1994)

Colorful Paper Flowers

In Mexico, fiestas and parades are filled with colors. Traditional costumes are bright and colorful, and a popular folk art is paper flowers. Paper flowers can be made out of almost any type of paper. In this activity, the students will make a version of paper flowers, using tissue paper.

Materials: 18" x 3" (45 x 8 cm) strips of tissue paper (many colors), pipe cleaners

Directions:

1. Place four or five strips of tissue paper on top of one another. Pleat the strips going back and forth.

2. Once pleated, use a pipe cleaner to twist around the middle of the pleated papers.

3. Gently pull apart the layers of tissue on each side of the pipe cleaner to fluff the flower.

4. Use a pair of scissors to cut leaf shapes out of green tissue; secure with pipe cleaner.

Try experimenting with different types of paper (such as crepe paper, tissue, art paper) and different sizes of paper strips to make different sizes of flowers.

Fold tissue back and forth, accordion style.

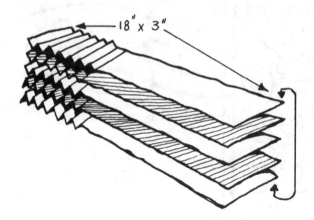

Tie strips in the middle.

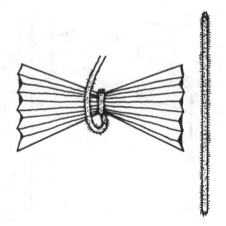

Separate layers and fluff out.

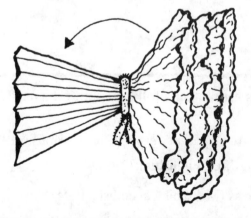

Cut leaf shapes. Secure with pipe cleaners.

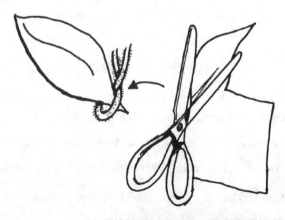

Joan Baez

Folk Singer and Political Activist _____

In Joan Baez's autobiography, _And a Voice to Sing With_, she attributes her initial interest in singing to loneliness. She was born on January 9, 1941, in Staten Island, New York. Her mother was Scottish and her father, Mexican. She was the middle child among three daughters. Her parents became Quakers and instilled in Joan her commitment to nonviolence. Her father received his Ph. D. from Stanford and began what could have been a lucrative career as a research physicist at Cornell University. Because of his moral concerns and religious beliefs, Albert Baez turned down military defense work at Cornell. As a result, the family moved several times in order for her father to find work.

As a young child, Joan Baez experienced discrimination and loneliness. She was rejected by Anglo children because of her dark skin and Mexican name, and she was also rejected by the Mexican children because she did not speak Spanish. Joan Baez's main interest in high school was singing in the choir. She worked on developing her voice and learned how to play the ukulele.

After Joan graduated from high school, the Baez family moved to Boston. She enrolled at Boston University, and she and a roommate began singing folk songs at local coffee houses. She soon went solo and began singing at a Harvard Square jazz club.

By 1959, she recorded her first album, _Folksingers Round Harvard Square_. The same year she was invited to sing with a popular folk singer, Bob Gipson, at the Newport Jazz Festival. She received many offers for recording contracts and concert appointments. Joan Baez chose to sign her recording contract with a small recording company, Vanguard, that was committed to quality, classical recordings. She preferred to perform concerts at small auditoriums, outside concerts, and college campuses. She actively protested the Vietnam War and has been involved in many political and social concerns.

Since 1973, she has been involved in Amnesty International, and in 1986 she participated in an Amnesty International concert called "Conspiracy of Hope" along with musicians such as Sting, U2, and Peter Gabriel. She founded Humanitas International in Menlo Park, California, an organization that promotes human rights and nonviolence. Joan Baez continues to perform benefit concerts, and her activism has not decreased in a career that has spanned more than thirty years.

Suggested Activities

1. **Folktales.** Joan Baez is known as a folk singer. Read some American folktales and listen to some American folk songs. Why are they called "folk" tales and songs?

2. **Buñuelos (A Special Treat).** Every country has its own traditions, and in Mexico the tradition of Noche Buena is celebrated. Noche Buena, or Christmas Eve, is a special time in many Mexican homes. On La Noche Buena, "good" children receive a special food treat called buñuelos.

   However, buñuelos are a tasty treat anytime of the year. All you need is an electric skillet, vegetable oil, flour tortillas, sugar, and cinnamon.

   • In a small container mix sugar and cinnamon and put aside.

   • Heat oil until hot (about 350° F, 180° C); use enough oil to cover tortillas completely.

   • Fry tortillas until crisp (about 30 seconds each side).

   • Drain on paper towel. Sprinkle with cinnamon and sugar and serve.

   • Tortillas can be cut into wedges before frying or served whole.

3. **Breads.** Tortillas are the kind of bread that many Hispanics traditionally eat. Go to your local supermarket and see how many different kinds of bread products you can find. From what ethnic groups do they come? Try different kinds of breads such as pita bread, tortillas, crumpets, matzo, French bread, etc.

4. **Children's Song.** The following is a children's echo song that you can try singing to the tune of "Frère Jacques."

   Buenos Días, Buenos Días   **Good Morning, Good Morning**
   ¿Como estás? ¿Cómo estás?   **How are you? How are you?**
   Muy bien, gracias,   **Very well, I thank you**
   Muy bien, gracias   **Very well, I thank you**
   ¿Y tu? ¿Y tu?   **And you? And you?**
   (Y is pronounced with the long e sound.)

Recommended Reading

From Sea to Shining Sea: A Treasury of American Folk Tales and Folk Songs by Amy L. Cohn (Scholastic, Inc., 1993)

Tortillas Para Mamá by Margot C. Greigo et al. (Henry Holt & Co., 1988)

Ojo de Dios (God's Eye)

An ancient tradition of the Huichol of Jalisco, Mexico, Ojo de Dios (God's Eye) weavings are good luck symbols believed to bring good fortune and health. The Huichol believe in the gods of nature. The crossed sticks that serve as the frame symbolize the four universal forces: earth, fire, water, and air. Colors have special meanings as well. Blue or turquoise represents the rain, green is fertility, yellow represents the sun, and brown is for the earth.

An Aztec legend tells of a beautiful princess who was born blind. The gods promised to restore her vision if anyone could duplicate the eye of God. One day, the sun's rays reflected a rainbow into the princess' tears. Using several yarns, her mother reproduced the colorful pattern. As soon as the weaving was complete, the princess regained her eyesight.

Materials:

- 2 sticks (Twigs, dowels, tongue depressors, or craft sticks can also be used.)
- several colors of yarn
- scissors

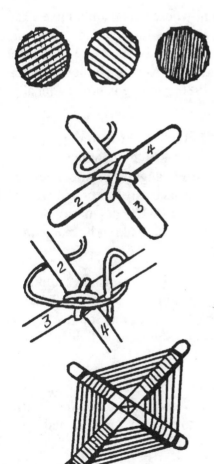

Directions:

1. Select three colors of yarn and wind each into a small ball.

2. Choose the color to be placed in the center of the "eye."

3. Number the spokes counterclockwise from one to four. Spoke #1 must be at the top, spoke #2 to the left, and so on.

4. Hold the structure in the left hand at a point close to where the sticks intersect.

5. Holding the ball of yarn in the right hand, bring the yarn around spoke #1, going around from the back side. (See the illustration.)

6. Yarn will always wrap from the left side of the top spoke, travel around the back and come out from the right side of the top spoke.

7. Rotate the sticks clockwise so that spoke #2 is now at the top and spoke #1 is on the right.

8. Bring the yarn around spoke #3, going from the left side and around.

9. Rotate the sticks again clockwise so that spoke #3 is at the top and spoke #2 is on the right.

10. Continue the technique of rotation, wrapping until the desired width of the center eye is achieved. To change colors, cut the yarn ball and firmly tie the next color of yarn to the end and continue wrapping.

Amado Maurilio Peña

Storyteller and Artist

Amado Maurilio Peña was born in 1943 in Laredo, Texas. His family descends from a mixed Yaqui Indian and Chicano background. As a young boy, he had a talent and love for drawing. He went to college at Texas A. & I. and received his bachelor's degree in sociology in 1965. In 1971 he received his master's degree in art and education. Peña taught in South Texas and Austin, all the while doing what he loved best, drawing. His art became more popular in the 1980s, and he is now nationally known. He know makes his living as an artist.

Peña's art is seen everywhere on posters, greeting cards, tiles, and T-shirts. He is certainly recognized throughout the Southwest. He uses a variety of mediums, including acrylics, in paintings and drawings. His particular motif which distinguishes his art from others is a modeled, angular profile. He depicts a profiled Indian face in much of his art. His original work is what appeals to art lovers and critics. The proliferation of his work to posters was a business decision on Peña's part. The popularity of his posters has extended his art and made it more accessible to the public while making his name more highly recognized.

Peña explores themes such as woven blankets in a variety of forms, including drawings, paintings, etchings, monotypes, and lithographs. He uses models and photographs in conjunction with the theme he is working on. Because he wants his art to tell the story of people's lives in the Southwest, Peña makes frequent use of the profile. Many of his works of art have been tributes to individual family members and friends.

According to Amado Maurilio Peña, success has meant that he is able to do and enjoy the things that are important to him, as well as to share his experiences with others. According to *Southwest Art*, when people ask him how long a particular painting took, Peña likes to answer, "an hour and a lifetime."

Suggested Activities

1. **Southwestern Art.** Look at books or collect pictures from magazines of Southwestern art. Ask students to examine carefully the samples and to name the attributes that would classify a piece of art as Southwestern. What is the motif common throughout?

2. **Mexican Pottery.** There is a valley in the state of Jalisco, near Guadalajara, Mexico, where the finest Mexican pottery is made by hand and with a potter's wheel. Use clay or hardening bread dough to make sculptures or figures. Paint your sculpture using Southwestern designs.

3. **Art Gallery.** Visit your local museum or art gallery. What kind of art appeals to you and why? Experiment in the classroom with different art forms such as drawing, painting, collage, sculpture, etc. What form of art do you prefer to create? Why?

4. **Lacquer Art.** Lacquer is an art form that was arose in Mexico prior to the Spanish conquest. The process begins by lacquering a black background on wood and allowing it to dry. A design is then cut into the lacquer with a fine point, and color is applied one color at a time. Students can simulate their own lacquer art using 6-inch (15 cm) or 9-inch (23 cm) paper plates. Use wax crayons to color a multicolored design that covers the whole paper plate. Leave no space white and press very hard with the crayons. The coloring should be thick and cover the entire surface of the plate. Use black tempera paint and brush over the entire plate. Allow to dry and brush with a glue and water mixture to finish.

Recommended Reading

Fiesta by Beatriz Zapater and José Ortega (S & S Trade, 1993)

Exciting Things to Make with Wool, String, and Thread by Rosalind May (Lippincott, 1977)

Folk Art Traditions by Bobbi Salinas-Norman (Pinata Publications, 1987)

Mexican Sand Painting

In Mexico there are artists who are known for their sand paintings in which they actually use fine-colored sand to create beautiful pictures. The following activity is a variation on the same theme.

Materials:

- 30 squares of sandpaper
  (approximately 5" x 5" 13 cm x 13 cm)
- multicolored crayons

- plain white paper
- iron
- old towel

Advance Preparation:

- Cut sandpaper squares (if not purchased pre-cut).
- Cut white paper squares slightly larger than sandpaper squares.

Lesson Directions

1. Students draw a picture on sandpaper square, using as much of the space as possible and using as many different colors as possible. 	2. Place sandpaper drawing on white paper, face down. Place in between folds of an old towel and iron on medium high heat for about 10 seconds until the crayon melts. 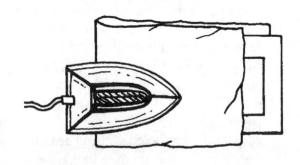
3. Allow to cool, then carefully peel back sandpaper, and the drawing will have transferred to the paper. 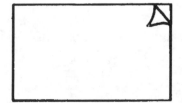	4. Frame picture on a piece of colored construction paper. 

Experiment with different grades of sandpaper and different textures of white paper.

Luis M. Valdez

Playwright

Luis M. Valdez is perhaps best known as a playwright and dramatist. He wrote and produced a play called _Zoot Suit_ in 1978 which was later made into a movie, and he created El Teatro Campesino, the farm workers' theater. _Zoot Suit_ is the first play written by a Mexican American playwright to reach Broadway. He also wrote and directed the film _La Bamba_.

On June 26, 1940, in Delano, California, Luis M. Valdez was born into a migrant farm worker family. He was the second eldest of ten children. His family moved from town to town in the San Joaquin Valley of California, following the various crop harvests. He attended many schools throughout the central valley and graduated from James Lick High School in San José, California.

In 1960, Valdez received a scholarship to San José College (now San José State University), where he majored in English and mathematics. He had always been interested in drama, and in the drama department at San José State he produced his first full-length play, _The Shrunken Head of Pancho Villa_, in 1963. He graduated in 1964 with a B.A. in English.

In October, 1965, Luis M. Valdez went back to his birthplace, Delano, and joined Cesar Chavez and his work with the farm workers' union. Valdez created El Teatro Campesino, the farm workers' theater, which put on acts or skits to entertain the striking grape workers. He used the theater, with no props, scripts, or stage, to educate the farm workers and the general public. He continued to broaden the scope and purpose of the theater by going on a national fundraising tour. He moved the theater, and now cultural center, to Fresno, which is centrally located in California, in an attempt to bring its message to more people.

In 1971, El Teatro settled in San Juan Bautista, California, a mission town, in a complex called Teatro Calaveras. Luis M. Valdez has received many honors and awards, including an Emmy and three Los Angeles Drama Critics' Circle Awards. The Committee on Arts and Humanities honored him in 1983, and the next year he was selected as a Regent's lecturer in theater at the University of California in Irvine. Linda Ronstadt appeared on PBS in Valdez's, _Corridos_ in the fall of 1987. Most recently, he directed a film for which he wrote the script, _Viejo Gringo,_ based upon a novel by Carlos Fuentes.

Suggested Activities

1. **Zoot Suit.** Luis M. Valdez is well known for his play *Zoot Suit*. In the 1930s and 1940s in Los Angeles, there was a mixture of youth who considered themselves neither Mexican nor American. The boys dressed in baggy zoot suits and wore their hair in "ducktail" cuts. Many had tattoos. The girls wore short skirts, bobby socks, and makeup. There was a lot of hostility directed towards them, and they were discriminated against for being different.

    Read about the Sleepy Lagoon Case (1944) and the Zoot Suit Riots (1943) in Los Angeles, California.

2. **Puppet Show.** Make different kinds of puppets to dramatize short stories. Students could choose a fairy tale to dramatize for younger students or write an original play with a contemporary theme. Students can make paper bag puppets or use paper plates attached to tongue depressors. For ring puppets, cut a strip of paper 2½" x 1" (6.3 cm x 2.54 cm). Overlap and glue the ends together to make a ring. Cut out circles the size of quarters and draw a face in each circle. Glue a face on each ring and slip it on your finger. For glove puppets, cut off the fingers of an old rubber glove and use fine felt pens to decorate the fingertips.

3. **Puppet Stage.** Make a puppet stage. Use a large rectangular cardboard box and remove one of the larger sides. Cut a large opening on the opposite side for the stage front. Staple stage curtains to the inside of the stage opening. Place the stage on a table and add a table skirt to make the puppeteers invisible to the audience. Use this stage when delivering your puppet show created for the previous assignment.

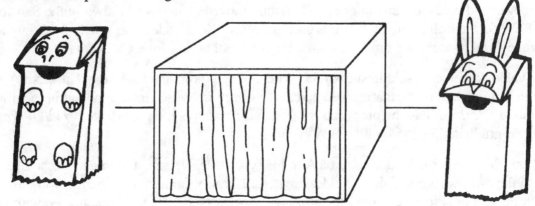

4. **Education of Actors.** Like Luis M. Valdez, a lot of actors and actresses went to college before entering the spotlight. Find out more about your favorite actors or actresses. Have they gone to college? Did they have any other occupations before they became famous? How long did it take before they were famous?

Recommended Reading

Vejigante: Masquerader by Lulu Delacre (Scholastic, 1993)

Mermaid Tales from Around the World by Mary Pope Osbourne

Where Angels Glide at Dawn: New Stories from Latin America

Writing a Script

Luis M. Valdez is a famous playwright. Work with a group of three to six students and write a script for the following folktale. After writing the script, make puppets and act out the story for your classmates.

The Horse and the Bee

Once upon a time a horse and a bee decided to have a race.

The horse said, "You silly bee! Of course I'll win the race. I am so big and strong and fast. You are just a little tiny bee."

A bee replied, "Don't be so sure of yourself, horse. I might be a little tiny bee, but I'm very smart. I think I can win the race."

All the animals were invited to watch the race between the bee and the horse. "Poor bee," some said, "he doesn't have a chance." The rule was that whoever crossed the finish line first was the winner.

It was time for the race to begin. "Ready, set, go!" The horse started running. Quickly the bee hopped onto the horse's tail. As the horse ran and ran, the bee slowly crawled up its tail. Next the bee crawled across the horse's back, over its head, and finally, down its nose.

The horse was reaching the end of the race, getting closer to the finish line, and he looked back to see the bee. "Ah ha!" he thought to himself, "I have won the race!"

Just then the bee got to the end of the horse's nose and crossed the finish line first.

"I win, I win, I win!" buzzed the bee.

Carmen Zapata

Actress and Dancer

Carmen Zapata showed interest in music and dance when she was a little girl by playing the piano and violin and by singing and acting at school. Although her mother disapproved of her interest in being an actress, she struggled to provide dancing and singing lessons for Carmen. Carmen Zapata has received countless awards, not only for her acting but also for her civic efforts and commitments.

For twenty years she performed in musicals on Broadway, and in between plays she performed at night clubs. She appeared in such Broadway musicals as _Oklahoma_ and _Guys and Dolls_. She had an extensive career in television and starred in more than three hundred programs. In 1973 with only $5,000, Zapata, along with Cuban director Margarita Galban and designer Estelo Scarlata, opened the nonprofit Bilingual Foundation of the Arts.

The goal of the Bilingual Foundation of the Arts is to bring Hispanic culture and experiences, through bilingual theater, to Spanish and English speaking audiences. On different nights the performances alternate between English and Spanish versions, which makes the theater unique and which appeals to a wide variety of audiences. Carmen Zapata works closely with the Los Angeles Unified School District to make Hispanics in the arts accessible and known to the students.

As a child coming from a Spanish speaking home, Carmen's first school experience was difficult. She did not speak English, and she was thrust into the mainstream classroom and a school culture that was foreign to her. Even though she was born and raised in the Spanish Harlem section of New York City and spoke only Spanish at home, Carmen felt that she did not know much about Mexican culture as a child.

Carmen Zapata is often called "The First Lady of the Hispanic Theater." Her awards include the 1984 Best Actress Award for dramatic performance and a local Emmy award in 1973 for a documentary. She has received numerous awards for her activism, including the most prestigious Civil Order of Merit in 1990 from His Majesty Juan Carlos I, King of Spain.

Suggested Activities

1. **Mexican Dance.** Try this simple dance called "Baile de los Viejitos" (Dance of the Old Ones) that is performed for the Day of the Dead. Dancers hobble to the dance area, single file, holding their backs and bending their knees as if it hurts to walk.

Counts	Steps
2	Tap right heel on floor.
2	Tap right toe on floor.
2	Tap left heel on floor.
2	Tap left toe on floor.
Tap 3	Step right foot across left foot.
Tap 3	Step left foot across right foot.
Tap 5	Tap cane on floor.
Hold 3	Twist head right.
Hold 3	Twist head left.
Hold 3	Twist trunk right.
Hold 3	Twist trunk left.
Tap 5	Tap cane on floor.
Hold 3	Jump forward, feet together.
Hold 3	Jump backward, feet together.

Midway through the dance, "los viejitos" begin to jump around the dance with lots of energy, and then they resume the traditional steps. When the dance is over, they hobble out as they came in. Ask your local librarian for help in selecting a record or use your favorite music to try the dance.

2. **Comparison.** Attend a local production of a play, ballet, or dance. Compare the live production to television or video. How are they different? Alike? Which do you prefer? Why?

Recommended Reading

Arroz Con Leche by José Luis Orozco (Scholastic Inc., 1994)

Early Stages: The Professional Theater and the Young Actor by Walter Williamson (Walker, 1986)

Famous Mexican Americans by Janet Morey and Wendy Dunn (Dutton, 1989)

Cognate Words Activity

A *cognate* is a word that appears to be the same word in two languages and has the same meaning in two languages. Spanish and English have many words that are similar. Some words are borrowed from one language by the other, and some words are similar because the English and Spanish languages share common roots in Latin.

Below are listed some cognates in English and Spanish. Try covering up the English list and look only at the Spanish list first. Can you guess what the English word will be? What do the words mean? Write the definitions in the space provided.

English	Spanish	Meaning
alphabet	alfabeto	_____
animal	animal	_____
artist	artista	_____
car	carro	_____
chocolate	chocolate	_____
confusion	confusíon	_____
conversation	conversacíon	_____
elephant	elefante	_____
flower	flor	_____
guitar	guitarra	_____
impossible	imposible	_____
Indian	indio	_____
insect	insecto	_____
invisible	invisible	_____
jelly	jalea	_____
penguin	pinguino	_____
poem	poema	_____
terrible	terrible	_____
tiger	tigre	_____
train	tren	_____
universal	universal	_____
zoo	zoológico	_____

José Antonio Burciaga

Muralist

José Antonio Burciaga's parents emigrated to the United States from Mexico. He was born in El Paso, Texas, in 1940. His mother had been a teacher in Mexico, and she encouraged him in his schoolwork and instilled in him a love of reading. As a child, he had a great interest in drawing and art, and he read constantly, particularly biographies and novels. At the age of twenty, Burciaga joined the air force and served three years in Spain and one year in Iceland. After his service in the air force was complete, Burciaga returned to Texas.

At this time, José Antonio Burciaga took his first art classes at the University of Texas at El Paso. He graduated in 1968 with a degree in fine arts and commenced to work as a graphic artist for the civil service. He also worked for the Central Intelligence Agency in Washington, D. C.

In the 1970s, Burciaga moved to California and began exhibiting his art. He took part in the Chicano art movement in the Bay area, and he increased his writing. In 1977 he gained publicity for one of his murals. Burciaga and a fellow artist were commissioned to paint a mural on the side of a building in Redwood City, California. The mural was entitled "Danzas Mexicanas" and took much hard work and creativity to complete.

At the public dedication ceremony, Burciaga noticed that in the program the Arts Council and all the sponsors of the mural were named, but the program failed to recognize the artists themselves. When it was Burciaga's turn to go to the podium to speak, he abruptly turned and threw a splash of paint over the mural. The crowd gasped! Ironically, the mural was so colorful and complex that looking at it later, one could scarcely notice the paint splash.

In addition to his art and writing, Burciaga served as project director for the Multicultural Task Force for the San Mateo Arts Council. He did illustrations and cover art for Macmillan Publishing Company. Burciaga wrote essays about the Chicano experience for the Hispanic Link New Service.

In 1988 José Antonio Burciaga published many of the essays in a book entitled, *Weede Peepo*. His writings are lighthearted but serious and combine humor and commentary. He recently published a book entitled *Drink Cultura*. José Antonio Burciaga now lives and works at Zapata House, Stanford University, Palo Alto, California.

Suggested Activities

1. **Aztec History.** Aztec history and roots are an important part of Chicano identity for José Antonio Burciaga. In the thirteenth century the Aztec empire flourished in Mexico. The Aztecs are well known for their intricate and detailed calendar called the Aztec Calendar or Sun Stone. Read more about the Aztecs and their way of life.

2. **Murals.** Some murals are made by adding paint to wet plaster. Make your own mural, using a disposable, rectangular aluminum pan. Pour plaster of Paris into an aluminum pan and allow to dry for about twenty minutes. The plaster should be somewhat set but still damp. While you are waiting for the plaster to dry, draw on a piece of paper the design that you will paint on your mural.

    Use tempera paints to paint your mural, the more colors, the better. Allow the plaster to dry for at least one hour before taking it out of the aluminum pan. Display.

3. **Local Murals.** Call your local Arts Council or Chamber of Commerce and ask about existing murals in your community. Go and visit a mural, if possible.

4. **Bark Painting.** Another type of Mexican handicraft is a bark painting. Artisans paint designs directly on tree bark. You can make your own bark painting by using a brown paper grocery bag and tempera paints. Use fine-pointed brushes for detail, if possible. Tear a rectangular piece of brown paper bag and tear off the edges to give a rough finish. Crumple the paper into a ball several times and then smooth it out. Draw a design lightly with a pencil (birds, lizards, small animals, flowers). Paint the design and let it dry. After the paint is dry, take a dry brush and brush the background to give it a rough leather look.

    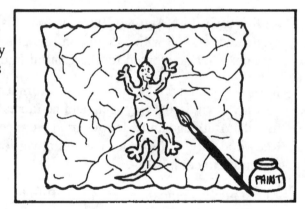

Recommended Reading _____

Undocumented Love by José Antonio Burciaga (Chusma House, 1992)

Neighborhood Odes by Gary Soto (HB Juvenile books, 1993)

The Hispanic Americans by Milton Meltzer (Harper, 1982)

Plata Azteca

Aztec Indians were known for their magnificent silver jewelry designs, and some very old Aztec designs are copied today by artisans. Some Mexican artists are famous for the silver jewelry and other silver pieces that they create.

One silver jewelry technique involves hammering the silver to create a raised relief or impression on the other side. Here is an easy way to achieve the same effect.

> To make your own *plata Azteca* (Aztec silver) piece you will need these materials: cardboard, thick string or cord, yarn, white glue, scissors, aluminum foil, hole punch.

Directions:

1. Cut the cardboard to the size and shape that you want.

2. Create an original linear design (such as a sun or moon, pyramid, abstract, etc.) with pencil on the cardboard piece.

3. Cut pieces of heavy string or cord and glue on the cardboard, following the lines of the design.

4. Allow the glue to dry completely.

5. Cut a piece of foil larger than the cardboard. Place the foil over the cardboard, covering the cord. Gently push down the foil around the cord, creating a raised relief.

6. Turn the edges under and glue to the back of the cardboard. Punch a hole at the top and string with yarn to wear as a necklace.

Cut a cardboard shape.   Create a design.   Glue on heavy cord.

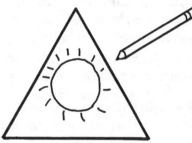

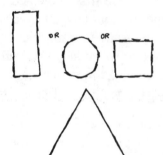

Cover with aluminum foil.   Secure foil on back with tape.

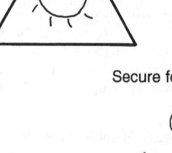

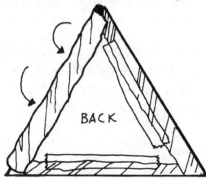

Angela de Hoyos

Bilingual Poet _____

Angela de Hoyos was born in Coahuila, Mexico, on January 23, 1945. When she was only three years old, she suffered a terrible accident. De Hoyos was burned by a gas heater and was confined to bed as she healed. She had severe burns on her neck and chest, and the smoke that she inhaled from the fire caused respiratory problems. It was then, as she suffered in bed, that she began making up rhymes. Her mother encouraged her interest in poetry. Angela de Hoyo's father had a dry cleaning business that he abandoned soon after the accident, and he moved the family to San Antonio, Texas.

In San Antonio, Angela de Hoyos attended local schools, and her poems were first published in her high school newspaper. Some of her poems were then published in literary journals, and she was ready to embark upon her writing career. De Hoyos did not take the traditional route of a four-year university degree program. She decided to follow her own course of study and took classes at several universities in fine arts and writing. At the same time, she became interested and involved in the Chicano movement. She continued educating herself and writing, as well as giving readings of her poetry.

By now, de Hoyos had written a sufficient number of poems to publish her collections. Her first collection, *Arise, Chicano: and Other Poems*, was published in 1975. The poems center around the theme of empowerment of Chicanos and the fight to overcome oppression. As a young girl, and later as an adult, Angela de Hoyos experienced firsthand the prejudicial treatment of which she writes. Her second book was also published in 1975 and is a collection of poems entitled *Chicano Poems for the Barrio*.

In her second book and her subsequent publications, *Selecciones* in 1976, and *Woman, Woman* in 1986, de Hoyos chose to use the Spanish language as the major language in her poetry. She interweaves English and Spanish in her poetry. Through her poetry she encourages Chicanos to empower themselves and to preserve their Chicano culture.

Suggested Activities

1. **Poetry.** Name your favorite poem. Who is the author? Why is it your favorite? Why does it appeal to you? Memorize your poem and recite it to the class. Read other poems by the same author.

   Have students create their own nature poems. The suggested style of poetry for poems about nature would be Haiku. Have students use the information and writing space on page 42 to write their poems.

   After the students have completed their poems, have them create a Mexican Tree of Life and display their poems beside the trees. Directions for the Tree of Life are provided on page 109.

2. **Think/Pair/Share.** Use the cooperative learning strategy called think/pair/share for the following questions. Students first think about the questions themselves, next they share with a partner, and, finally, any set of partners can share with the larger group.

   Imagine what it would be like to live in the United States if you could not speak English at all. Or, pretend that you can speak only a little English and you have to repeat things before people understand you.

   > What would it be like?
   > How would you feel?
   > Has anyone ever made fun of the way you talk?
   > How did you feel?
   > What did you do?
   > What could you do to make someone with limited English feel better?

3. **A Multicultural Debate.** Do you think that people in a multicultural society should all speak the same language? Why or why not? Try to come up with strong arguments for both sides. With your teacher's help, form debate teams and have a debate over this controversial subject.

4. **Average American.** Do you have a mental image of an "average" American? Write a paragraph and draw a picture of him or her. Read your paragraph and ask yourself whether your average American is a male or female? How old? What does he/she look like? Where does he/she live? What does he/she do for a living? Most importantly, where does your image come from?

Recommended Reading

Fire in My Hands by Gary Soto (poems) (Scholastic, 1992)

Where the Sidewalk Ends by Shel Silverstein (poems) (Dell, 1986)

Taking a Walk: Caminando by Rebecca Emberely (bilingual book) (Little, 1990)

The Hispanic Americans by Milton Meltzer (Harper, 1982)

You Can Be a Poet Too!

Haiku is a Japanese form of poetry that is unrhymed and has only three lines. The first line has five syllables, the second line has seven syllables, and the third line has five syllables. Read the following example. Then choose a topic and use words in Haiku poetry form to describe your topic. Write your poem in the bar below.

Rain

dripping, sprinkle, drop
tapping on my window pane
splish, splash, splish, splash, drop

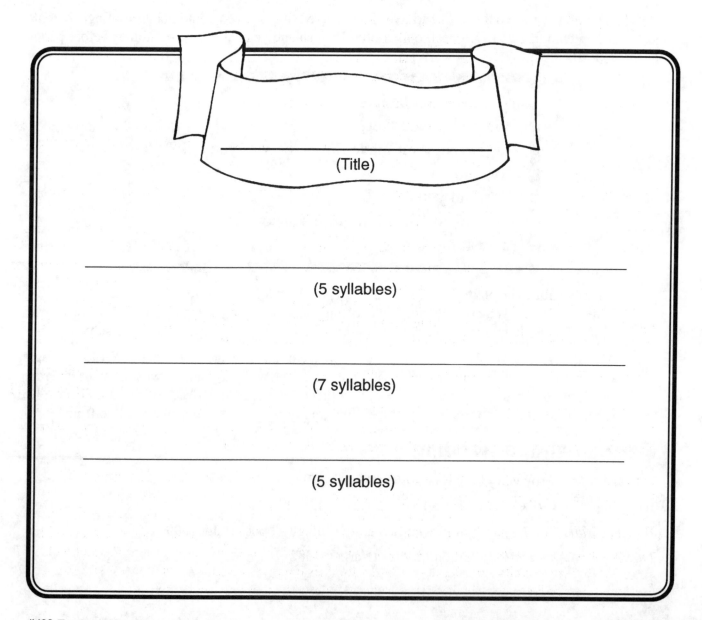

_____
(Title)

_____

(5 syllables)

_____

(7 syllables)

_____

(5 syllables)

Gloria and Emilio Estefan

Musicians and Activists _____

Gloria Maria Fajardo was born on September 1, 1957, in Havana, Cuba. Concerned for the safety and well being of his family, Gloria's father took his family to Miami when Cuba was overthrown by Fidel Castro. Gloria's father was very much interested in politics. He took part in the Bay of Pigs and also joined the military during the Vietnam War. However, when he returned from military service, his health began to fail, and the burden of caring for her father soon fell upon Gloria at the young age of eleven. Her mother was working as a teacher to support the family.

In 1952 Emilio Estefan was also born in Cuba. The Estefans owned and operated a factory and did not leave Cuba until six years after Castro took over. At the age of thirteen, Emilio and his family traveled to Spain and then finally emigrated to the United States. In 1968 he was offered a job as a mail clerk at Bacardi Imports and by 1980 held the position of Director of Latin Marketing.

Emilio had loved music since he was a young boy. Now that he was settled in a stable job as mail clerk, he decided to take up music. After playing solo in restaurants and parties, Emilio formed a group, The Miami Latin Boys, in 1974. They played at private parties and weddings. In the meantime, Gloria Fajardo was finishing high school and preparing to enter the University of Miami. She attended a family wedding with her family where Emilio and The Miami Latin Boys were the entertainment. At the wedding the band invited her up on stage to sing a few songs with them. Eventually, Emilio asked Gloria to become part of the band. Gloria was reluctant at first because she was concerned about her studies at college. Finally, after asking permission from her parents, Gloria agreed to sing with the band. She continued to study hard at the University of Miami, and she also held a part-time job.

The band changed its name to The Miami Sound Machine and was popular among Hispanics in the United States as well as all over Latin America. In 1978, Gloria received her degree in psychology and communications from the University of Miami, and Emilio was still working for Bacardi. They had been dating now for two years, and on September 1, 1978, Gloria's twenty-first birthday, they were married. The Miami Sound Machine also released its first album that same year.

Between 1981 and 1983, the group recorded and released four more albums in Spanish for CBS Records. In 1984 their first English language album, _Eyes of Innocence_, was released, and in 1985 the hit song _Conga_ appeared on their album _Primitive Love_. The success of the group continued. They released several more albums in the following years, and both Gloria and Emilio were nominated for and received several music awards. Along with their growing success was their commitment and service to the community. In March of 1990, Gloria Estefan was congratulated at the White House by President George Bush for her work in warning youngsters about the dangers of drugs.

Suggested Activities

1. **Latin Music.** Go to your local library and listen to other Latin music albums by artists you may or may not have heard of. What does all Latin music have in common? Can you differentiate all of the different instruments? How is Latin music different from other American music? How is it the same?

2. **Just Say No.** Gloria Estefan is very active in getting young people to say no to drugs. Join in the campaign. Make signs for your classroom and your school to promote a drug-free school and community.

3. **Fidel Castro.** Both Gloria and Emilio Estefan left Cuba because of Fidel Castro. Find out more about Cuba and Fidel Castro. Where is Cuba located? Why did so many Cubans disagree with Fidel Castro? Who rules Cuba now? Draw a map of Cuba.

4. **English and Spanish.** Like many other bilingual artists, Gloria and Emilio Estefan record music in both English and Spanish. Why do you think they continue to record in both languages? What other artists do you know about who record songs in two languages? Why do you think this is important?

5. **Miami.** Many Cubans who left Cuba went to Miami. Study the population diversity of Miami. How many Cubans now live in Miami? How is Miami dealing with the multicultural population? What are some of the cultural festivities that you might see when visiting Miami?

Recommended Reading

The Cuban Americans by Renee Gernard (Chelsea House Publishers, 1988)

The Bossy Gallito: A Traditional Cuban Folktale by Lucia Gonzales (Scholastic Inc., 1993)

Coming to North America from Mexico, Cuba, and Puerto Rico by Susan Garner and Paula McGuire (Dell, 1981)

Recommended Listening

Mi Tierra by Gloria Estefan (a tribute to her Cuban roots)

These Are the Days by Gloria Estefan (released in 1994)

Maracas

The Indians in Mexico long ago used many instruments such as drums, flutes, gourds, and shells to play music. Maracas, a type of instrument that originated long ago, are still used today.

Activity
Use the materials below and follow the directions to make your own maracas.

Materials:
- 2 soda pop cans, cleaned and dry
- 2 unsharpened pencils
- tape
- wallpaper scraps or construction paper
- seeds or pebbles

- markers
- glue
- hammer
- large nail

Directions:
1. Put several pebbles or seeds in the soda pop can. To prevent the pebbles or seeds from spilling out, temporarily place a piece of tape on the open end of the can as you work on the maracas.

2. Use a hammer and nail to punch a hole in the center of the bottom of each soda pop can.

3. Push the unsharpened pencil through the bottom hole of the can.

4. Poke the end of the pencil through the hole in the top of the can so that the end of the pencil sticks out no more then ¹/₂ inch (1.25 cm). To prevent the ends of the pencil from slipping out of the can, secure them with tape.

5. Decorate your maracas with scraps of wallpaper or construction paper.

   Enjoy the sounds and rhythms you can produce with your homemade musical instruments.

Hispanic Art—Huichol Nierikas

Hispanic art is commonly vibrant, colorful, bold, and open. The art is like a song, rich in melody and diverse in sound. An art form developed in Mexico that influenced Hispanic American artists uses colorful yarns to create pictures. Yarn painting is not an ancient craft but an adaptation from an old tradition. A *nierikas* is a wooden offering covered with yarn in designs representing requests to the gods. The Huichol of Mexico adapted this into a two-dimensional craft. To make a nierikas, beeswax is coated onto the surface of a flat wooden board. A pointed stick is used to draw the design on the wax. Strands of yarn are then pressed into the wax to outline the shapes. More strands of yarn are pressed close together to fill in each shape and the entire background area. The designs for the nierikas are a blend of fantasy and reality, using bright colors and swirling yarn patterns. Animals, snakes, corn, and the sun are popular images.

Materials:

- 6" (15 cm) square piece of cardboard
- pencil
- thin, colorful yarns
- glue
- scissors

Directions:

1. Draw a large shape in the center of the cardboard square.

2. Roll the desired yarn colors into small individual balls.

3. Select a yarn color to outline the shape. Apply glue to the pencil line and then press yarn on top of the glue. Cut off remaining yarn.

4. Select a second color of yarn. Apply glue to the center of the design and attach the end of the yarn as illustrated.

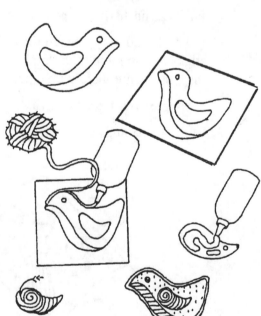

5. Fill in the center area with the yarn glued in a circular direction. The strands of yarn should be pressed close together.

6. Apply more glue to the area as needed. Continue to fill in the rest of the shape with yarn until the yarn meets the outlined edge.

7. After the center shape is completely filled in, begin to cover the background area with yarn, using the same technique but with a different color of yarn.

8. To create a border around the picture, select another color of yarn and glue at least two rows around the edges.

Questions to Promote Thinking

1. Why did José Antonio Burciaga throw paint upon his own mural? What message was he trying to deliver?

   _____

   _____

   _____

2. What do you think Amado Maurillo Peña meant when he said that a painting took him "an hour and a lifetime" to create?

   _____

   _____

   _____

3. Why do you think that Angela de Hoyos combines the English and Spanish languages in her poetry?

   _____

   _____

   _____

4. Describe a time when you felt disappointed.

   _____

   _____

   _____

   _____

5. Describe an accomplishment of yours for which you feel especially proud.

   _____

   _____

   _____

   _____

Science and Medicine

Below is a listing of Hispanic Americans represented in this section. Following each name is the Hispanic American's country of origin and brief statement about his or her achievements.

Hispanic American	Country of Origin	Achievements
José Andrés Chacón	U.S.A.	engineer and columnist
Dr. Antonia Novello	Puerto Rico	former Surgeon General of the United States
Franklin Chang- Diaz	Costa Rica	physicist and astronaut
Dr. Francisco Bravo	U.S.A.	rancher, businessman, doctor, and founder of Bravo Clinic
Ellen Ochoa	U.S.A.	astronaut and inventor

José Andrés Chacón

Engineer and Aviator

José Andrés Chacón is an engineer who received his Ph. D. from George Washington University in business administration. He writes a syndicated column called "The Minority No One Knows." Previously he worked as an administrator for a large corporation and served in the military and Peace Corps.

In 1925, José Andrés Chacón was born in a small town, Peñasco, south of Taos, New Mexico. He was the eldest of six sons. He grew up in New Mexico during the Great Depression, and he attended Catholic schools. When he was in senior high school, Chacón became interested in aviation. He later joined the U. S. Navy, and in World War II he served as an aerial gunner in the Pacific.

After World War II, he had the opportunity to go to West Point. At West Point he received his bachelor's degree in engineering and was commissioned to serve in the Korean War as a second lieutenant. He served as a navigator-bombardier and was awarded the Distinguished Flying Cross at the end of his service in Korea.

After his military service, José Andrés Chacón worked for the Sandia Corporation, which was a contractor to the Atomic Energy Commission. He also served as the director of a Peace Corps project, the Cooperative League of the United States, in Peru. He later served on the President's Commission on Mexican American Affairs and as an officer in the Equal Employment Opportunity Commission.

Suggested Activities

1. **Newspaper Critique.** Dr. Chacón is a columnist, and usually columns and editorials are known to reflect the perspective of the authors. However, you may find it interesting to analyze your local newspaper for bias and perspective. Begin by critically reading the first section of the newspaper and answer the following questions.

> - How many people mentioned in the stories are male? female? How can you tell?
> - How often do people of minority groups appear? in negative stories? in positive stories?
> - How much space is devoted to each person mentioned? Compare.
> - Are most of the reporters male or female? Do male and female reporters cover different kinds of stories?

2. **News Broadcast.** Have students develop their own set of critical questions to analyze the news broadcasts on your local television stations.

3. **Perspective.** The following art activity deals with perspective. Find a large photo (preferably full page) of a person's face from a magazine. These photos can usually be found in women's magazines in the advertisements. Fold the picture of the face exactly in half symmetrically and cut off one half. Glue one half on a paper and use pencils, markers, crayons, etc., to draw the other half. You can also do the same exercise with pictures of objects, but faces are quite interesting.

4. **The Peace Corps.** José Andrés Chacón served as the director of a Peace Corps project in Peru. Explain to students that the Peace Corps is a United States government independent overseas program. The men and women volunteers work with people in developing countries to improve their living conditions. Have students bring in articles from the newspaper or magazines which feature information about countries in need of assistance. Discuss how organizations like the Peace Corps can help. Ask students to work in groups to write their own set of goals for such organizations.

Recommended Reading

Kids Explore America's Hispanic Heritage by Westridge Young Writers Workshop (John Muir Publications, 1992)

Good Neighbors? The United States and Latin America by Ann Weiss (Houghton-Mifflin, 1983)

Behind the Headlines at the Big City Paper by Betty Lou English (Lothrop, 1985)

Wanted!

José Andres Chacón writes a column titled "The Minority No One Knows." In the space below, choose a student in your school that you know well but maybe someone else in the class does not. This student can be older or younger. Draw a picture of the student and then fill in the information below. Exchange "Wanted!" papers with a friend and see whether he/she can find your mystery person and you can find his/hers.

(Draw picture here.)

Name_____

Height _____   Weight _____

Hair _____   Eyes _____

Hobbies are_____

Often can be found_____

Favorite subject in school _____

Special talents_____

Who am I? _____

Dr. Antonia Novello

Surgeon General

When Dr. Antonia Novello was appointed Surgeon General of the United States in 1990 by President George Bush, she vowed to be an advocate for women and children. Dr. Novello was particularly concerned with those who had been infected with AIDS and also with those teenagers with drinking problems.

Dr. Novello was the first woman and the first Hispanic to be considered for the job of Surgeon General, and she already had a reputation for dedication and hard work. After she was appointed, Dr. Novello told the Washington Post in an interview that ". . . as a woman, as a Hispanic, as a member of a minority, . . . I bring a lot of sensitivity to the job."

On August 23, 1944, Antonia Novello was born in Fajardo, Puerto Rico. She and her brother were raised by her mother, Ana Flores Coello, who had a great influence on Novello's career. Antonia wanted to become a doctor because she was concerned about others who suffered as she had as a child. Until she had surgery at age eighteen, Novello suffered from a painful illness of the colon (part of the digestive system).

After receiving her B. S. and M. D. from the University of Puerto Rico in 1970, she began her internship and residency in pediatrics at the University of Michigan Medical Center in Ann Arbor, Michigan. At that time, it was difficult for women to be accepted in the field of medicine. However, she was well respected by her classmates, and in 1971 she was the first woman to receive the University of Michigan's Pediatrics Department's Intern of the Year Award.

Before she was appointed Surgeon General, Dr. Novello held many important positions. She was on the staff at Georgetown University Hospital in Washington, D. C., as a pediatric nephrology fellow. She served at the National Institutes for Health. She also earned a master's degree in public health from Johns Hopkins University in 1982. From 1986 to 1990, Dr. Novello continued her work concerning children by working as the deputy director of the National Institute of Child Health and Human Development.

Shortly after becoming Surgeon General, Dr. Antonia Novello went back to her birthplace, Puerto Rico, and was greeted by children lining the streets and handing her flowers. After she spoke at the Veteran's Administration Hospital, she told the Washington Post that " . . . I have to be good as a doctor, I have to be good as Surgeon General, I have to be everything."

Suggested Activities

1. **Women in Office.** Read about other women in office such as Joycelyn Elders (successor to Dr. Novello as Surgeon General of the United States), Roberta Achtenberg (Assistant to the Secretary of Housing and Urban Development, Henry Cisneros), Ruth Bader Ginsburg and Sandra Day O'Connor (Supreme Court Justices), Diane Feinstein and Barbara Boxer (California Senators), Carol Mosley Braun (Illinois Senator), and Donna Shalala (Secretary of Health and Human Services). Form cooperative groups to research the women mentioned above. Write short biographies about the women and transfer the biographies onto index cards. Separate the cards into an even number for each member of your group to use to report orally to the class.

2. **Who Am I?** After listening to the reports from all the groups in the class about the women in office, have students write a brief statement about the woman they researched on the back of an index card and her name on the front. These cards can then be combined to play a game of "Who Am I?" One person reads the statement, and the other person must guess who the woman is. Also, students could make a concentration game by writing the statement on one card and the woman's name on the other. Mix all cards together and lay cards turned over on the floor. Students must match the names of the women with the statements.

    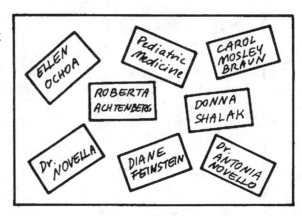

3. **Surgeon General.** Dr. Antonia Novello was appointed Surgeon General of the U. S. in 1990. Find out more about this office. What are the main responsibilities of the Surgeon General? What are the qualifications for the Surgeon General? Who is the Surgeon General now?

4. **Pediatrics.** Dr. Novella devoted much of her career to pediatric medicine. Survey students to find out how many have had such childhood illnesses as chicken pox, mumps, measles, rubella, etc. Point out that many of these illnesses are now preventable due to the efforts of scientists and doctors who have dedicated their life's work to the improvement of children's health. Have students research some of the more common childhood illnesses to learn the history of the illnesses and the progress made in eliminating disease.

Recommended Reading

Famous Puerto Ricans by Clarke Newton (Dodd, Mead, & Co., 1975)

The Hispanic Americans by Milton Meltzer (Harper, 1982)

Famous Mexican Americans by Janet Morey and Wendy Dunn (Dutton, 1989)

Solidarity by Anna Sproule (Watts, 1988)

Health and Science by Jenny Bryan (Hampstead, 1988)

Advertising

In late 1991, Dr. Antonia Novello met with some of the largest beer and wine companies in the United States. She asked them to stop aiming their advertisements at children and teenagers. She was also concerned about cigarette advertising.

Look for a cigarette or alcohol advertisement in magazines that you think may appeal to young people. Cut out the picture or draw your picture in the space provided. On the lines below, write an explanation of why you think the ad appeals to young people. Do you think this is appropriate or responsible advertising? Why or why not?

_____

_____

_____

_____

Franklin Chang-Diaz

Physicist and Astronaut

Franklin Chang-Diaz dreamed of being an astronaut when he was a little boy in Costa Rica. He and his friends would pretend that a big cardboard box was their spaceship and they were all astronauts. As a boy Franklin Chang-Diaz would look up into the night sky, trying to see the trajectory of Sputnik, the first satellite that was set into orbit by the Soviet Union in 1957. Years later, Franklin Chang-Diaz's dreams of becoming an astronaut came true when he became the first Hispanic astronaut in NASA.

After graduating from high school, Franklin Chang-Diaz left Costa Rica and moved to the United States to live with a Costa Rican family while he went to college. The astronaut corps had just been established, and Chang-Diaz still had dreams of being accepted. He worked to pay his way through school. He earned his B. S. in mechanical engineering from the University of Connecticut. He continued in graduate school and received his Ph. D. from M. I. T. in 1977 in the study of plasma physics.

In 1980 Franklin Chang-Diaz joined the space program as a physicist. After completing the training program for the astronaut corps, the astronauts are usually assigned technical jobs. They are assigned to a support group. When considering the astronauts to go into space for a mission, NASA takes into consideration not only whose turn it is to go but also what specific skills the person has that will match the needs of the mission. Usually, the average time between recruitment and the astronaut's first space mission is four years.

Finally, Franklin Chang-Diaz's dream came true. In 1986, he went up in the space shuttle Columbia. His job was to conduct scientific experiments. He also helped compile information regarding deployment of a satellite that was carried by the shuttle.

Chang-Diaz spends much time making appearances and talking to school children. He especially encourages Hispanic children to become interested in and pursue an education in the sciences.

Suggested Activities

Franklin Chang-Diaz studied physics in his efforts to become an astronaut. According to *Webster's Dictionary*, physics is "a science that deals with matter and energy and their interactions in the fields of mechanics, acoustics, optics, heat, electricity, and magnetism..."

Have students try some of the experiments below and on page 57.

1. Rocket to the Moon

Materials: 15 feet (450 cm) of string, two chairs, plastic drinking straw, tape, and a long balloon

Directions:

- Tie one end of thread to the back of a chair. Slip a plastic straw over the free end of the string, then tie this end to another chair. Move the chairs apart to the opposite sides of the room so that the string forms a taut line.

- Drape three 4-inch (10 cm) pieces of tape over the straw as shown. The ends should hang loosely on each side.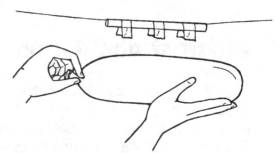

- Blow up a long balloon and pinch the opening closed. Press the balloon against the straw so that the tape sticks to the balloon on each side.

- Release the balloon by taking your fingers away from the opening. The balloon will rocket along the string.

- Discuss what happened. (The air in the balloon is under pressure. As the air escapes from the back opening, the thrust causes the balloon to shoot forward along the path of the string.)

2. Superman and Wonder Woman

You will need a broom and a friend. Ask a friend to turn sideways and hold both hands straight out and grasp the broom handle. Place one of your hands in the center of the broom handle between your friend's two hands with your arm bent at the elbow, grasping the broom handle with a downward tug. Tell your friend that you bet that he or she cannot push you over. As your friend pushes the broom towards you, push straight up. You will remain standing in place.

Discuss what happened. (You have much more leverage with one bent arm acting as a lever than your friend has with two straight arms.)

Recommended Reading _____

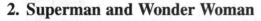

Space Exploration & Travel by Louis Sabin (Troll Assocs., 1985)

Projects in Space Science by Robert Gardner (Julian Messner, 1988)

Scientists and Technologists by Irene M. Frank and David M. Brownstone (Facts on File, 1988)

Physics Experiments

Crack Me Up

Materials: one raw egg, your bare hand

Directions:

1. Make sure that you are not wearing any rings or have any hard objects in your hand. Hold a raw egg in your hand.

2. Now squeeze your hand closed as hard as you can. Do not be afraid. The egg will not break!

What happened?

When you squeeze an egg in your hand, the force is spread over a large area, and the egg can withstand this force because it is shaped like an arch. An arch is very strong and is often used in construction. When you crack an egg the normal way, you hit it on the side against an edge of something so the force is concentrated and the shell breaks.

Super Paper

Materials: one sheet of copier paper, rubber band, book

Directions:

1. Roll the paper into a tube and secure loosely with a rubber band.

2. Stand the tube on end on the table top and carefully place a book on top. You will notice that the paper tube can support the book.

What happened?

A tube has much more strength than a flat object. That is why pillars, which are tube shapes, are used in buildings to hold up weight.

Paper Power

Materials: sheet of paper, scissors, your two hands

Directions:

1. Make two slits at the top of a piece of paper. Use both hands to hold the paper at the top edges.

2. Try to pull outward with a slow steady force so that you have three separate pieces of paper. You will not be able to tear it in three pieces, only two.

What happened?

As you apply force, the weakest spot begins to tear first. Then all of the force is applied to that spot until it is completely torn. The other two strips remain attached.

Dr. Francisco Bravo

Businessman and Doctor

Dr. Francisco Bravo was born in 1910 in Santa Paula, California. His parents were Mexican immigrants, and as a teenager he had to work after school to help support his family. During the summers, his family followed the harvest and worked in the farm fields.

After he completed high school, Bravo entered the University of Southern California and studied pharmacy. He supported himself through college by working different jobs and by continuing his summer farm work.

After he graduated, Dr. Bravo got a job as a pharmacist and continued to go to school at the University of Southern California. He got his Master's Degree in sociology and then decided that he wanted to study medicine. He went to Stanford University to study medicine for six years and received his M. D.

When he went back to Los Angeles, Dr. Bravo opened his private practice. He also opened a free medical clinic for Mexican Americans, the Bravo Clinic. He wanted to encourage young Mexican Americans to go into the medical fields, so he established scholarships for students of Mexican descent.

Besides medicine, Dr. Bravo has been involved in many community and philanthropic affairs. He was one of the founders, president, and chairman of the board of the Pan American Bank in East Los Angeles, an area of Los Angeles where businesses were needed.

Interestingly, Dr. Francisco Bravo is also the owner of a 1,500 acre farming operation in Southern California. In his agricultural enterprise he raises hogs, cattle, citrus, and grains. He is also involved in real estate development. Because of his many roles in business, he has been called upon to serve on numerous medical, civic, and governmental committees and boards.

Suggested Activities

1. **California Crops.** As a youngster, Dr. Bravo worked in the farm fields of California, and as an adult he established his own agricultural enterprise. Research all the different crops that are grown in California. On a California map, draw a picture of each crop in the area it is grown.

2. **Dealing with Being Different.** Not only do students of migrant farm working families struggle to keep up in their school work, but they also are often the subject of teasing and ridicule at school. Have students recall situations where they have seen classmates making fun of a student who was "different" from them in some way. What did you do? If you ignored the incident, imagine how the student felt. Ask students to imagine how the person would have felt if a classmate had stepped in and taken his or her side.

   Ask students to think about the situation so they can be ready to deal with it the next time they are confronted with it. Have them write down three solutions to this situation.

3. **Grouping.** Dr. Bravo not only practices medicine as a doctor, but he also involves himself in many other areas, especially community outreach. Have students discuss the groups they or people they know belong to. Ask them to briefly describe the purposes and goals of the groups. Have students contact Social Services or other community service organizations in the area for information on their programs. Ask students to use the information received to complete the outline on page 65. Share responses in class.

   As an alternative, ask students what kind of community outreach program they would like to establish if they had the opportunity to start one. As a class, brainstorm ways to initiate such a program in the community. Consider such questions as these: Where should the headquarters be? What are the goals of the program? How do we encourage community participation? What steps do we take to "reach out" to members of the community in need of our services?

4. **Common Threads.** Encourage a class discussion about the similarities and differences among people. Talk about attributes, habits, etc., and ask students to point out some common threads people share in interests, talents, likes, and dislikes. Then, distribute page 60 and have students work in groups to complete the activity. Discuss each group's responses.

Recommended Reading

A Migrant Family by Larry Dane Brimner (a story about 12-year-old Juan Medina and his family that reveals the hardships and uncertainties of migrant family life) (Lerner Pub., 1992)

Hello, Amigos! by Tricia Brown (a story of a Mexican American boy who lives in the Mission District in San Francisco, California) (H Holt & Co., 1992)

Home Before Dark by Sue Ellen Bridges (Knopf, 1976)

Neldo by Pat Edwards (Haughton, 1987)

Common Threads

Form groups of four for this activity. Take turns asking each other questions about likes and dislikes, attributes, habits, etc. For example, do you like pizza? Do you wash the dishes at home? Do you have a brother?

Each person has his or her own outer rectangle in which to list categories that pertain only to that person. For example, if you are the only one in the group with a bicycle, write it in your rectangle. The square in the middle is for the commonalities of the group, so if you all like ice cream, write it in the square.

Commonalities

Ellen Ochoa

Astronaut and Inventor

Not only is Ellen Ochoa an astronaut, she is also an inventor who has three patents for her work in optical processing. Ellen Ochoa also has many hobbies, such as playing the flute, playing volleyball, bicycling, and flying. She became the first Hispanic woman astronaut in 1990. Ellen Ochoa wants young girls to know that if they work hard enough, their dreams for the future can come true.

Ellen Ochoa was born in Los Angeles, California, and her father was of Mexican descent. Her parents divorced when she was in junior high school, and Ellen grew up in La Mesa, California, with her mother and brothers and sister. Her mother always encouraged her to do well in school, as did her older brother. Not only did Ellen's mother encourage her, she also set an example by taking college classes herself for many years, and she finished her degree with a triple major.

When Ellen Ochoa was in high school, she worked very hard to do well. She went to San Diego State University where she received her bachelor's degree in physics. At Stanford University Ellen earned a master's degree and a Ph. D. in electrical engineering. Even after becoming an astronaut, Ellen Ochoa has remained involved in research, and at the young age of thirty-two, she holds three patents for optical processing that she developed.

As an astronaut, Ellen Ochoa is often asked to speak to young people. She encourages students, especially young girls, to study math and sciences. She also says that her hard work helped her to achieve her goal of becoming an astronaut, and she urges young people to work hard at whatever they do.

Suggested Activities

1. **Survey.** Traditionally, women, and especially women of color, were not encouraged to study math and sciences. Yet many women overcame societal pressures and excelled in untraditional fields.

   Survey your classmates to find out how many boys and girls enjoy math and how many boys and girls enjoy science. Write your results in the form of a percentage. Write your results in the form of a fraction. Write your results in the form of a decimal. Make a graph to show your results. Speculate about why the results turned out the way they did.

2. **Graphing.** Brainstorm all the different kinds of graphs (for example, bar graphs or Venn diagrams). Talk about how different graphs are more conducive for different sets of data. Form cooperative groups and have each group come up with a survey question for their classmates.

   After collecting their data, see whether each group can graph their results using a different kind of graph (line graph, bar graph, pictograph, pie graph, or Venn diagram).

3. **Women in Math and Science.** Discuss reasons why women were not traditionally encouraged to study the sciences. Discuss difficulties women may have faced in pursuing careers in math and science. Research famous women or minorities who were successful scientists and mathematicians.

4. **Weightlessness.** As with all astronauts, Ellen Ochoa experienced the sensation of weightlessness. During weightlessness, objects appear to have no weight and they "float" effortlessly within the capsule. Explain to students that this phenomenon occurs when a spacecraft is in orbit and gravity is trying to pull the craft back to earth. The speed of the spacecraft carries it forward. As the spacecraft is being pulled by gravity and moves forward at the same time, so does the astronaut. This experiment will help students visualize weightlessness. For each group of three students, you will need thread, scissors, a glass jar, and a small doll.

   Procedure: Tie a piece of thread around the neck of the doll. Tie two pieces of thread opposite each other around the mouth of the jar. Connect them to the thread, holding the doll as shown. One person holds the upper end of the thread while standing on a desk or table and releases the jar to a second person standing on the floor ready to catch it. The third person observes. Switch roles so each student can be an observer.

Recommended Reading

Women and Numbers by Teri Perl (Wide World Publishing, 1993)

Mothers of Invention by Ethlie Ann Vare and Greg Ptacek (William Morrow & Co. 1988)

The Worker in America by Jane Claypool (Watts, 1985)

Venn Diagram

Use the following Venn diagram to survey your classmates about their interests in math and science. Design other Venn diagrams to survey your classmates about other subject areas. On a separate paper, report your findings in a well-written paragraph.

Likes math

Likes science

Likes math and science

Who's Who?

Create a game that tests your memory of who's who in this section. In each box below, write a fact about one of the Hispanic Americans you studied. Use four boxes for each person. Cut out the boxes and use them as game cards. Turn each card over and write the name of the person to whom the fact refers. With the name side face down, read a fact and name the person. If you are correct, keep the card. Alternate turns. When all cards are picked up, the player with the most cards wins.

Fact	Fact	Fact	Fact
Fact	Fact	Fact	Fact
Fact	Fact	Fact	Fact
Fact	Fact	Fact	Fact
Fact	Fact	Fact	Fact

Service Organization Report Outline

Many prominent people in the fields of science and medicine volunteer their time to local or national organizations created to improve the human condition. Contact a community service organization in your area. Find out the answers to the following questions. When you complete this outline, share your responses with the class.

Name of Organization: _____

Address: _____ Phone Number:_____

1. Who are the people helped by this organization?

    _____

    _____

2. What services does this organization offer?

    _____

    _____

3. Is there a fee to be paid for the services offered?

    _____

    _____

4. How does a person go about getting help from this organization?

    _____

    _____

5. Is there anything else important to know about this organization?

    _____

    _____

Sports

Below is a listing of the Hispanic Americans represented in this section. Following each name is the Hispanic American's country of origin and a brief statement about his or her achievements.

Hispanic American	Country of Origin	Achievements
Rodolfo "Corky" Gonzales	U. S. A.	*Golden Gloves champion boxer, businessman, and community organizer*
Nancy Lopez	U. S. A.	*professional female golfer; named Women's Pro Rookie of the Year*
Lee Trevino	U. S. A.	*professional golfer*
José Canseco	Cuba	*Professional baseball player*
Roberto Clemente	Puerto Rico	*professional baseball player; voted into the Baseball Hall of Fame*

Rodolfo "Corky" Gonzales

Boxer and Community Activist_____

Rodolfo "Corky" Gonzales was born in 1929 in a Mexican barrio in Denver, Colorado. His parents were seasonal farm workers, and as in many poor farm-working families, by the time Gonzales was ten years old he was working in the sugar beet fields alongside his parents.

Rodolfo Gonzales went to school in the Denver public school system and graduated from high school at the early age of sixteen. By then, he was working in a slaughterhouse.

Boxing was always a sport that fascinated Gonzales, and he saw it as a way to escape poverty. He began boxing competitively as a teenager. Boxing proved to be successful for Gonzales. He was a Golden Gloves champion, won sixty-five of his seventy-five fights, and at the end of his career, he was ranked as the third highest contender for the World Featherweight title.

In 1953, Gonzales left his boxing career to start his own business, but his love of boxing continued, and he later returned to boxing as a trainer of young fighters. Corky Gonzales focused his energies on the development of Chicano self-identity, especially among young people.

After opening his own business, Gonzales became active politically. He initiated a program called Crusade for Justice which promoted Chicano self-determination. He supported civil rights for Chicanos and Indians, and he supported the efforts of Cesar Chavez. Gonzales organized and participated in demonstration marches concerned with civil rights issues.

In 1967, Rodolfo "Corky" Gonzales wrote a poem entitled "Yo Soy Joaquin," which was a high point in his career and also a significant contribution to the Chicano movement. Rodolfo "Corky" Gonzales is known and respected as a businessman, community organizer, political activist, and Chicano leader.

Suggested Activities

1. **Contemporary Sports.** The top three favorite sports among Latinos are soccer (called football in all other parts of the world), baseball, and boxing. Read about contemporary Latino boxers such as Julio Cesar Chavez and Oscar "Macho" Camacho. Consult the sports page of your local newspaper for more information or go to your local library.

2. **Children's Games.** All cultures have their traditional children's games. Here are two games from Mexico that are fun at any age.

Toro, Toro

Make a circle with one person in the middle who is the "toro" (bull). Children in the circle say, "Toro, toro, are you ready?" and the "toro" says, "No, first I must put on my" (names an article of clothing). Each time the toro must pretend to put on the article of clothing that he/she has said.

The children continue to call out, "Toro, toro, are you ready?" and the toro continues to say no and put on clothing until he surprises the group by saying, "Yes, here I come!" The toro chases, and the children run to the safe area (designated ahead of time) before they are tagged. The first person tagged becomes the toro.

Mis Vecinos Me Encantan

(I Like My Neighbors)

This is like a version of musical chairs. Chairs are placed in a circle facing inward with enough chairs except for the person in the middle. The person in the middle says, "I love my neighbors, especially my neighbors who wear" (names an article of clothing; sweaters, for example). All the children wearing sweaters must jump up and run inside the circle with the person in the middle and try to get another chair. Whoever is left standing goes to the middle.

Recommended Reading

Look What We've Brought You from Mexico: crafts, games, recipes, stories, and other cultural activities by Phyllis Shalant

Record Breakers of Pro Sports by Nathan Aaseng (Lerner, 1987)

The Hispanic Americans by Milton Meltzer (Harper, 1982)

Career Choices

Rodolfo "Corky" Gonzales was not just a boxer; later in his life he also became a businessman, community organizer, political activist, and Chicano leader. Think about what you want to achieve after high school. Do you think you will choose one career only, or would you like to keep your options open and try many different careers? On the lines below, write four possible career choices that you would like to explore. Investigate these careers further either by talking to someone in that field or using reference books in the library. For each choice, write one reason why you would like to pursue this career and one obstacle which may hold you back from reaching your goal. This will help you make a decision about where to start. Good luck!

Career Choice #1 _____

_____

_____

_____

_____

Career Choice #2 _____

_____

_____

_____

_____

Career Choice #3 _____

_____

_____

_____

_____

Career Choice #4 _____

_____

_____

_____

_____

Nancy Lopez

Professional Golfer

Nancy Lopez was born in Torrance, California, in 1957 while her parents were there visiting relatives. She actually grew up in Roswell, New Mexico, with her older sister, Delma, and her parents, Domingo and Marina. Nancy's father, Domingo, loved baseball and was a good player. He was even offered a tryout in the minor leagues, but family responsibilities came first and he gave up his dreams of baseball in order to support his family.

In 1964, Marina, Nancy's mother, became ill with a lung disorder. The doctor recommended that she walk outside daily to strengthen her lungs. Marina thought that simply walking everyday would be boring, so she suggested that she and Domingo play golf together for her daily exercise. The only problem was what to do with Nancy. Nancy's sister, Delma, was already married and living in California, and it would be too expensive to hire a babysitter. Nancy tagged along with her parents to the golf course and the making of a champion had begun.

Little by little, Nancy would ask to participate in her parents' golf games. Her father taught her how to swing the club and hit the ball. When her father saw how interested she was in golf, he spent hours giving her golf lessons. When she asked for clubs of her own, her mother gladly gave hers to Nancy. When Nancy was nine years old, she won the state of New Mexico Pee Wee tournament, scoring well enough to win the junior competition. However, the officials said that she was not old enough yet.

By the age of eleven, Nancy was invited to play in the New Mexico Women's Amateur Tournament. Nancy's father was very protective of her. He was concerned about her facing such competition at a young age, but she did well and was the runner up in the tournament. Her parents sacrificed and supported Nancy greatly. Her father was at her side, coaching her during practice, and her mother sewed her golf outfits. Her father even made a sand trap in the back yard because the local municipal golf course did not have one.

Nancy had her share of obstacles to overcome. The local country club would not sponsor her because she was Mexican American, and people often criticized her style. Lee Trevino, a famous Mexican-American golfer, encouraged her, and her parents worked hard to afford her the opportunity to go on tour. In 1977 she was named Women's Pro Rookie of the Year, and her success has grown ever since.

By 1995, she was the holder of 47 professional tournament championships and a member of the LPGA (Ladies Professional Golf Association) Hall of Fame.

Suggested Activities

1. **Golf Terms.** Have students find out what the following golf terms mean: *round, tee, teeing ground, driver, iron, rough, fairway, putter, par, wood, cup, putt, address, shank, bogey, ace, flag, sand trap, eagle, double bogey, putting green.* See if the students have any terms that they know or have found to add to the list.

2. **Categorizing.** After defining the words in activity one, ask students to put the words in categories (put the words that belong together in groups). Ask students to explain their categories (students will probably have different answers).

3. **Creative Writing.** Using the golf terms, have students write a story about an imaginary golf game and how well they played on each hole.

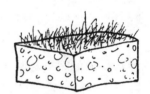

4. **Design a Course.** Golf courses are designed to be challenging to the golfer. Course designers use a variety of sand traps, water hazards, curves in the fairway, trees, and varying distances to the holes to make the game more exciting. Design your own golf course with eighteen holes and a clubhouse. Make sure each hole is labeled with its par.

5. **Sponge Golf Course.** Have students grow grass on sponges. Then place sponges together on a flat surface and add other features to create a miniature golf course. To make the sponge grass, you will need several sponges of the same size and the following materials: sewing needles, thread, craft sticks, grass seed, clean spray bottle, and water.

Directions: thread a needle. Tie the end of the thread to the middle of a craft stick. Push the needle and thread through the center of the sponge so that the craft stick rests at the base of the sponge. This will prevent the thread from slipping through the sponge. Sprinkle the upper surface of the sponge with seeds. Hang the sponge golf course in a sunny window and spray it with water daily. Watch grass grow!

Recommended Reading

The Picture Story of Nancy Lopez by Betty Lou Phillips (Messner, 1980)

Golf by John Morgan (EP Publishing, 1978)

Notable Hispanic Women Diane Telgen and Jim Kamp, editors (Gale Research Inc., 1993)

Miniature Golf

Have you ever played golf? Even if you have not, it is possible to set up your own miniature golf game in your classroom or outside in a parking lot or field.

Materials:

- golf clubs (3 – 4 per classroom)
- golf balls
- paper cups
- obstacles

Directions:

1. For this game you will need to clear an area in which to play.

2. Design a floor plan for your golf course in the space below.

3. Place paper cups on their sides in four different places around the area. Make sure they will not move, either by placing a small stone inside or taping them to the ground or floor.

4. Create obstacles by placing objects in the way of the paths.

5. You will play in teams of four. Each student plays a hole, and the team with the least number of strokes wins the game.

Lee Trevino

Professional Golfer

Lee Trevino was born in Dallas, Texas, in 1939. He was raised by his mother, Juanita, who worked as a maid, and his grandfather, Joe Trevino, who worked as a farmhand. When Lee was a little boy, he helped his grandfather pick cotton and worked in the onion fields. Lee's grandfather took him hunting for rabbits to provide meat for the family's dinners. When Lee was seven years old, his grandfather got a job as a gravedigger at a cemetery outside Dallas, where they moved into a small "house" with no running water, heat, or windows.

In this rural area, which years later became a suburb of Dallas, Lee noticed a green field where people were playing golf, although he did not know what golf was at the time. Lee soon discovered that he could earn some money by finding lost golf balls and selling them back to the golfers. When he was eight years, old, Lee became friends with the greenskeeper's son, and the two of them spent countless hours on the course when it was closed for business. The next job Lee got was as a caddie. His meager salary and his sometimes generous tips helped to sustain his family. He spent time with the caddies playing and practicing together with an old set of clubs which they shared and bet each other for quarters. Lee Trevino never really had any formal golf instruction; he was primarily self-taught.

Lee left school at the age of fourteen and was employed by Hardy Greenwood, who gave him a job at Hardy's Driving Range in Dallas. When Hardy's decided to expand and add a nine-hole course, Lee and another man designed and landscaped the whole twelve acres. At the age of seventeen, Lee Trevino joined the Marines. He continued to play golf as a Marine and was soon noticed by his superiors and reassigned to Special Services where he played full-time golf. When he was discharged from the Marines, he went back to work for Greenwood. He continued practicing and playing tournaments. By 1965, Lee Trevino was ready to try the Professional Golf Association (PGA) tour, but it was not until two years later that he finally got the opportunity. In 1968 he won his first big professional tournament, the U.S. Open.

In 1970 he led the PGA in earnings and went on to win a second U.S. Open and the Canadian and British Opens the following year. He was named PGA Player of the Year and Sportsman of the Year in 1971. In 1975 Lee Trevino was struck by lightning while playing the Western Open. After several back surgeries and rehabilitation, Trevino was back on the golf course. He has had great success and passed the two million dollar mark in earnings in 1979. He was elected to the PGA and World Golf Halls of Fame in 1981, and in 1990 he won seven of twenty-six PGA Senior Tour events. He can be recognized by his sombrero logo, and he has the nickname "Supermex."

Suggested Activities

1. **Lightning.** In 1975 Lee Trevino was struck by lightning on the golf course. That same day two other golfers were also struck by lightning but were not seriously injured. Several other golfers on the course had their clubs fly out of their hands. Ask students to research the phenomenon of lightning. Why are golfers particularly vulnerable? What are safety precautions to use during a storm with lightning?

2. **Research.** Research another famous Hispanic golfer, Chi Chi Rodriguez, who also got his start as a golf caddie. Find out if there are other similarities.

3. **Grass Person.** The game of golf is dependent on fairways and greens that are covered in well maintained and manicured grass.

   Directions:

   • Make your own "grass person."

   • Decorate a plain white Styrofoam cup with a marker or pen to look like a person's face.

   • Fill the cup three-quarters full with soil.

   • Sprinkle two teaspoons (10 mL) of grass seed on top and stir gently.

   • Water lightly and in about five to seven days your grass will begin to grow, making the hair for the face you drew on your cup.

   • Trim and groom as needed!

4. **Beginner's Book of Golf.** Provide reference materials for this activity. Have students work in groups to write handbooks for beginning golfers. They should include the general rules of golf and a glossary of important golf terms. As a challenge, have students write a page explaining how to swing a golf club. Ask other students to try to follow the directions on the page.

Recommended Reading

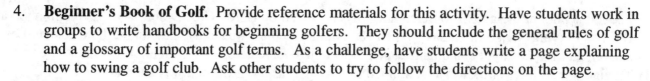

They Call Me Supermex by Lee Trevino (Random House, 1982)

Lee Trevino: Hispanics of Achievement by Thomas W. Gilbert (Chelsea House, 1992)

Golf: Plain and Simple by Don Trahan (Quinlan Press, 1986)

The Snake in the Sandtrap (and Other Misadventures on the Golf Tour) by Lee Trevino and Sam Blair (Holt, Reinhart and Winston, 1985)

The History of the PGA Tour by Al Barkow (Doubleday, 1989)

Design Your Own Course

Lee Trevino was part of a team that designed a nine-hole golf course. Now it is your turn to design your own golf course. Remember to design a course on which everyone will want to play. Your golf course should contain the following items:

Basic Elements of the Course

○ **9 holes**

a flag marking each hole

○ **greens**

the sections of the course where the grass is mowed very closely to the ground right around the holes

○ **fairways**

long stretches of land with mowed grass

○ **rough**

longer, unmowed grass alongside the fairways

○ **water**

small man-made lakes, streams

○ **sand trap**

a section of land dug out and filled with sand

○ **club house**

place where you sign up to play, sometimes have restaurants and golf shops

Use a large piece of white construction paper to design your course. Be sure to include a key to your map. Also, do not forget to give your course a title.

José Canseco

Baseball Player

José Canseco was born in Havana, Cuba, in 1964. He was raised in Miami, Florida. Until the age of 12, José and his twin brother, Ozzie, showed little interest in the sport. José played third baseman in high school, and was offered a college scholarship to join the American League's Oakland Athletics in 1982. However, he declined the offer.

Instead, José Canseco played on minor league teams until 1985. While in the minor leagues, José developed his strength through a vigorous weight-training program. By the end of the 1985 season, a 6-foot-3, 225 pound Canseco became a major league player. A year later, he had established himself as a power hitter and was named the American League's rookie of the year.

In 1988, José became the first player to steal 40 or more bases and to hit 40 or more home runs in the same season. For leading the majors in home runs, slugging percentages, and runs batted in, José Canseco was chosen the league's most valuable player.

Like many renowned sports figures, José was plagued with injuries. Despite his wrist and back problems, Canseco batted .357 in the 1989 World Series, which led to a team win for the Athletics. His success did not go unrewarded.

In 1990, the Athletics offered José Canseco a salary which made him the highest-paid player in baseball at that time. The offer included a five-year contract for $23.5 million. Canseco was also chosen to start in the All-Star Game in 1990, as well. He received more votes from fans than any other player.

José Canseco ranks among baseball's most reliable run producers. In the 1991 season, he had 152 strikeouts, 122 runs batted in, and 44 home runs.

José was traded to the Texas Rangers in October of 1992. His performance throughout his career has earned him the admiration of fans and a respected position in the world of baseball.

Suggested Activities

1. **Baseball Venn Diagram.** Baseball evolved from cricket. Have students work in groups to research the game of cricket. Compare the two games. In what ways are they similar today? In what ways are they different? Have each group prepare a Venn diagram to show these similarities and differences.

2. **Baseball Timeline.** The evolution of America's "national pasttime" is an interesting topic of research to many students. Students may work in groups or independently to research important dates and events in the history of baseball. Have them use the information they have collected to make time lines highlighting these events.

Sample of events that could be included in a timeline:

1857— Length of game to nine innings was established.

1869–1870— Cincinnati Red Stockings, first professional team, won 91 and
tied 1 of their first 92 games.

1901— American League declared itself a major league.

1933— Annual All-Star Game between teams' best players in each league
began.

1935— Night baseball introduced.

1947— African American players entered the majors.

---

3. **Baseball Terms.** Have students prepare a classroom chart of playing positions and common baseball terms such as *pitcher, catcher, umpire, runs batted in, errors, strike, home run,* etc. Add new terms to the chart as students locate information about baseball and baseball players.

4. **Baseball Graphs.** Divide students into groups and assign each a major league baseball team to research. Have groups prepare graphs representing the teams' wins and losses over a period of four years. (Use the same four years for each group.) Compare graphs representing each team.

5. **Baseball Math.** Distribute page 78 to students. Have them use the information to write baseball problems. When completed, have students exchange their baseball problems with a partner. Each student is to find the solutions to the problems.

Recommended Reading _____

Great Lives: Sports by George Sullivan (Macmillan, 1988)

Record Breakers of Pro Sports by Nathan Aaseng (Lerner, 1987)

Baseball's Hall of Fame by Harvey Frommer (Franklin Watts, 1985)

All About Baseball by George Sullivan (G.P. Putnam's Sons, 1989)

Baseball's Best: Five True Stories by Andrew Gutelle (Random House, 1990)

Baseball Math

Use the following facts to write five of your own math problems. Then, ask a partner to solve the problems. Prepare your problems on a separate sheet of paper, following the sample provided at the bottom of this page.

Baseball Facts

❖ Baseball is played on an infield and outfield. The infield is square, measuring 90 feet (27.4 m) on each side.

❖ Home plate is the corner farthest from the outfield. The outfield ends at an outer fence, which measures anywhere from 250 to over 450 feet (76 to over 137 m) away from home plate.

❖ The pitcher's mound is an 18 foot (5.5 m) circle. It lies inside a square 60 feet, 6 inches (18 m) from home plate.

❖ The defending players wear a leather glove. The catcher's glove, which is round and heavily padded, is the largest, measuring up to 38 inches (96.5 cm) in circumference and 15.5" (39.4 cm) from top to bottom.

❖ The player's bat can be up to 2.75 inches (7 cm) thick, and 42 inches (106.7 cm) long.

❖ A regulation baseball is 9 to 9.25 inches (22.9 to 23.5 cm) in circumference and weighs 5 to 5.25 ounces (141.7 to 148.8 g).

❖ The distance between bases measures 90 feet (27.4 m).

❖ The distance between home plate and second is 127 feet 3 ⅜ inches (36 m).

Sample

My Problem

Jim is a member of the Alban Little League team. He made three home runs for his team this year.

  a. How many feet did he run?

  b. How many yards did he run?

Solution

a. 4 x 90 = 360 feet

   360 x 3 = 1080 feet (answer)

b. 1080 divided by 3 = 360 yards
             (answer)

Answered by: Carl

Roberto Clemente

Baseball Player

Roberto Clemente loved baseball. As a young child growing up in Carolina, Puerto Rico, he played at every opportunity. While listening to the radio, he would squeeze a ball to build up muscles in his throwing arm. When he was in his bedroom, he would bounce a rubber ball off the wall to practice catching. When he and his friends were unable to buy real baseballs, they made their own from old golf balls, string, and tape.

As Roberto grew older, he practiced more and became a better baseball player. His first job playing baseball was with the Santurce Crabbers. Roberto was offered a job with the Brooklyn Dodgers, but his father said he had to finish school.

After completing his schooling, Roberto Clemente went to Montreal, Canada, to play on a farm team. He was soon discovered there by the Pittsburgh Pirates. They asked him to play right field for their team, and Roberto accepted.

As a Pirate, Roberto was on two World Series championship teams. He was the Most Valuable Player in the 1971 World Series. He had over 3,000 hits in his career. As a champion, Roberto never forgot his fans. To show his love for them, he thanked the fans instead of going to parties with his teammates. He donated money to people in need and he spent time visiting sick children. When an earthquake struck Nicaragua, Roberto Clemente spent the Christmas holiday collecting supplies for the victims. He was going to fly from Puerto Rico to Nicaragua on December 31, 1972, to deliver the supplies; however, shortly after the plane took off, it crashed. Roberto and everyone else on board died.

Roberto was missed by many people. Three months after he died, he was voted into the Baseball Hall of Fame. Roberto's father wanted him to be a good man. Roberto Clemente proved to be a great man.

Suggested Activities

1. **Biography Review.** After reading the biography on page 79, ask students to respond to the following questions.

   • Why do you think Roberto practiced baseball so much?

   • How do you think Roberto felt when his father would not let him join the Dodgers?

   • How did Roberto Clemente share his success?

   • What kinds of baseball players do you think are admitted into the Hall of Fame?

   • Why do you think Roberto Clemente was considered a great man?

2. **"Aspira."** Roberto Clemente grew up in Puerto Rico. Have students research to find out more about the history and traditions of the people of Puerto Rico. Explain that many Puerto Ricans believe in *aspira*. This word means "to strive." Explain the word to your students as you write it on the board. Ask the students what they strive to do. Perhaps they will say, "Making good grades," or "Finishing in the top ten of my swim team." Record all of their ideas. Then have each student write one paragraph explaining what he or she is striving for and another paragraph describing how he or she can achieve these aspirations.

3. **Festivals.** The people of Puerto Rico celebrate special occasions with festivals. Listed below are some Puerto Rican festivals held in the month of February.

February 5 - 7	*Orchid Festival*	Ponce, Puerto Rico
February 19 - 21	*Fish Festival*	Cabo Rojo, Puerto Rico
February 12 - 14	*Small Fish Festival*	Naguabo, Puerto Rico
February 21 - 28	*Coffee Festival*	Yauco, Puerto Rico

Make a large calendar for the month of February. Display it in the classroom. Introduce the festival and label its celebration date on the calendar. Add a symbol on the calendar to represent the type of celebration (fish for Small Fish Festival, flower for Orchid Festival, etc.).

Divide the class into groups and ask each group to research one of the festivals. Have students present their research to the class.

Recommended Reading

Roberto Clemente: Pride of the Pirates by Jerry Brondfield (Garrad Publishing Company, 1976)

Felita by Nicholasa Mohr (Dial Books, 1979)

Record Breakers of Pro Sports by Nathan Aaseng (Lerner, 1987)

Great Lives: Sports by Regge Sullivan (Macmillan, 1988)

Using Statistics

The following chart shows Roberto Clemente's statistics while he played for the Pittsburgh Pirates. Use the information to answer the questions that follow.

Year	Games	Home Runs	RBI	AVG
1960	144	16	94	.314
1961	146	23	89	.351
1962	144	10	74	.312
1963	152	17	76	.320
1964	155	12	87	.339
1965	152	10	65	.329
1966	154	29	119	.317
1967	147	23	110	.357
1968	132	18	57	.291
1969	138	19	91	.345

RBI = Runs Batted In   **AVG = Batting Average**

1. In what year did Clemente hit the most home runs? _____

2. In which season did Clemente have the highest batting average? _____

3. In which year did Clemente play the fewest games? _____

4. Did Clemente have more RBI in the first or second five years of the decade? _____

5. In what years did Clemente play the same number of games? _____

6. In what year did Clemente play the most games? _____

7. How many RBI did Clemente have in 1963? _____

8. What was Clemente's batting average in 1961? _____

9. How many games did Clemente play in 1969? _____

10. In which two years did Clemente have the fewest home runs? _____

Interviews and Introductions

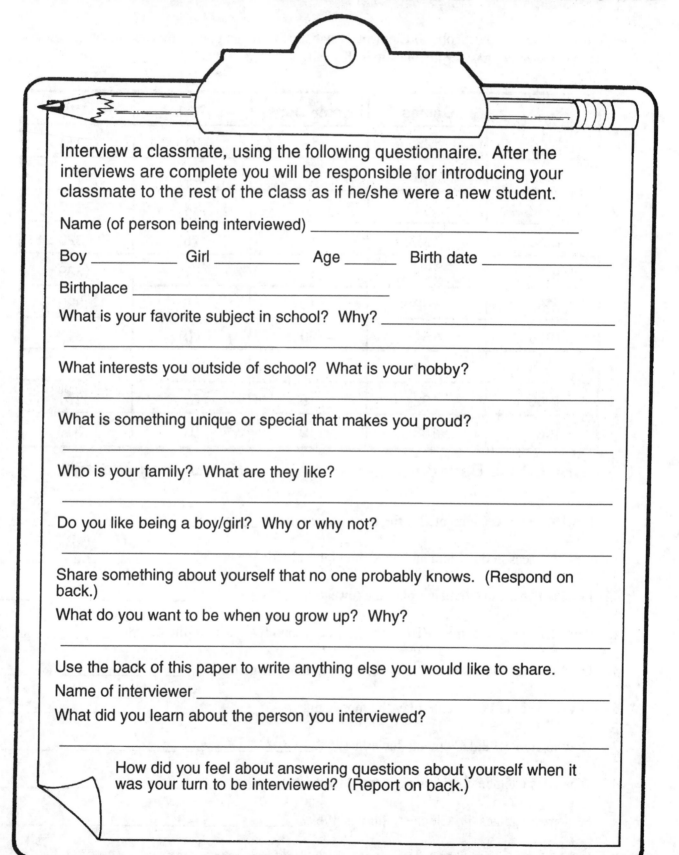

Interview a classmate, using the following questionnaire. After the interviews are complete you will be responsible for introducing your classmate to the rest of the class as if he/she were a new student.

Name (of person being interviewed) _____

Boy _____ Girl _____ Age _____ Birth date _____

Birthplace _____

What is your favorite subject in school? Why? _____
_____

What interests you outside of school? What is your hobby?
_____

What is something unique or special that makes you proud?
_____

Who is your family? What are they like?
_____

Do you like being a boy/girl? Why or why not?
_____

Share something about yourself that no one probably knows. (Respond on back.)

What do you want to be when you grow up? Why?
_____

Use the back of this paper to write anything else you would like to share.

Name of interviewer _____

What did you learn about the person you interviewed?
_____

How did you feel about answering questions about yourself when it was your turn to be interviewed? (Report on back.)

Civic Leadership

Below is a listing of the Hispanic Americans represented in this section. Following each name is the Hispanic American's country of origin and a brief satement about his or her achievements.

Hispanic American	Country of Origin	Achievements
Cesar Chavez	U. S. A.	leader, founder of United Farm Workers Union
Dr. Hector P. Garcia	Mexico	civil rights leader, founder of G. I. Forum
Vilma Martinez	U. S. A.	attorney and public speaker
Edward R. Roybal	U. S. A.	Congressman and community leader
Katherine Davalos Ortega	U. S. A.	former treasurer of the United States
Dolores Huerta	U. S. A.	labor leader and social activist
Frederico Peña	U. S. A.	Secretary of Transportation

Cesar Chavez

Founder of United Farm Workers_____

The life of a migrant farm worker can be harsh. Housing is usually inadequate and food can be scarce. Children often miss school to work beside their parents. Because of the poor living conditions and backbreaking labor, many migrant workers' health deteriorates by the age of thirty-five.

Cesar Chavez was born in Yuma, Arizona, on March 31, 1927. Cesar's father lost several businesses and then his 100-acre farm in the Great Depression, and the family moved to California to follow the crops. Cesar attended more than 30 schools before dropping out of school at the age of 15 to help support the family.

In 1952, Cesar began working for the Community Service Organization, going door to door at night to encourage people to register to vote. He became the National Director of the CSO in 1958. Cesar believed that farm workers needed a strong union to fight for their rights and left the CSO in 1962 to begin the United Farm Workers (UFW).

He began by driving from town to town, field to field, talking to the workers, and organizing them. By 1968, the union was involved in a bitter struggle with growers over the pesticides that were sprayed on crops and the conditions for workers. The UFW called a strike and asked people to show support by boycotting California grapes, wine, and lettuce.

An advocate of nonviolence, Cesar initiated a hunger strike on February 14, 1968, which drew media attention. People from all over the country boycotted products sold by the growers, and other unions called sympathy strikes. This finally forced several large growers to sign contracts with the UFW, and Cesar ended his fast after twenty-five days.

The UFW continued to fight for worker's rights against influential opponents in government and business, expanding to assist workers in other states. In 1988, Cesar again fasted for thirty-six days to alert the public to the danger of pesticides that not only harmed workers but that traveled on grapes to the consumer's table.

On April 23, 1993, Cesar Chavez died in his sleep. During Chavez's life, his efforts on behalf of farm workers were recognized by Senator Robert Kennedy, Reverend Jesse Jackson, and many other notable leaders.

Suggested Activities

1. **"Dichos."** Cesar Chavez was fond of dichos and used them often. *Dichos* are sayings that are passed down through families. They often give advice or teach a lesson. It is not always possible to translate dichos directly, but the meaning can be given. Here are a few dichos. What do you think they mean?

    "Del dichos al hecho hay mucho trecho."
    It is easier said than done.

    "El que no habla, Dios no lo oye."
    He that doesn't speak, God does not hear.

    "Con la vara que midas, seras medido."
    With the rod that you measure, you will be measured.

    What do you think Cesar Chavez meant by his dicho, *"Hay mas tiempo que vida"* (There is more time than life.)?

2. **Book Club.** Start a multicultural book club in order to learn more about others. Ask a teacher or librarian for recommendations on books to read. Everyone in the club could read the same book and then discuss it together, or you could choose a topic and read books related to the topic. You might invite people with experience in the topic you are reading about to visit your group.

3. **Bulletin Board.** Make a bulletin board called "Hands Around The World." Use a picture of the world as the centerpiece. Have students cut out four hands, each of different skin colors. On each hand the students will write words that describe themselves. For example, one may write smart, friendly, shy, athletic, etc. Attach the hands in a circle around the globe, facing outward.

Recommended Reading

The Kid's Guide to Social Action: How to Solve Problems You Choose and Turn Creative Thinking into Positive Action by Barbara A. Lewis (Free Spirit Publishing, 1991)

Kidstories: Biographies of 20 Young People You'd Like to Know by Jim Delisle (Free Spirit Publishing, 1991)

Kids with Courage: True Stories About Young People Making a Difference by Barbara A. Lewis (Free Spirit Publishing, 1992)

Hunger Strike

In order to get the attention of the growers, Cesar Chavez initiated two hunger strikes in his life. One lasted for twenty-five days and the other thirty-six days. Cesar Chavez believed in nonviolent strikes and was able to achieve a great deal through his strikes. Imagine you are the leader of an organization that is in great need of change. How will you get the attention of the people that you need to, to make a change? Like Cesar Chavez, you also believe in nonviolent demonstrations. Think of five different ways to bring about change and explain why you think they will bring about change.

Demonstration #1:

_____

_____

_____

Demonstration #2:

_____

_____

_____

Demonstration #3:

_____

_____

_____

Demonstration #4:

_____

_____

_____

Demonstration #5:

_____

_____

_____

Dr. Hector P. García

Civil Rights Leader

Dr. Hector P. García was born January 17, 1914, in a small town called Llera, in the state of Tamaulipas in Mexico. He was only a little boy when his family fled Mexico during the Mexican Revolution. His family crossed the Mexico-United States border, settling in Texas. His parents always emphasized the importance of education, and in 1936 he earned his bachelor's degree from the University of Texas. He continued his schooling and concentrated on medicine.

During World War II, Dr. García served as an officer in the Infantry, Engineer Corps, and Medical Corps. He served as a medical doctor in Europe. He was awarded a Bronze Star and six Battle Stars. When his service was finished he went into private practice in Corpus Christi, Texas.

Dr. García was concerned with the poor and prejudicial treatment that Mexican-American veterans were receiving at the local veterans hospital. As a result, in 1948 he established the G. I. Forum, an organization designed to protect the civil rights of veteran Mexican Americans.

In 1949 the G. I. Forum gained national recognition when the organization came to the aid of the family of Felix Longoria. Felix Longoria was a soldier killed in World War II whose remains were found four years after the war. The funeral home in Longoria's hometown of Three Rivers, Texas, would not allow the family to use the chapel because the veteran was Mexican American. The G. I. Forum intervened on behalf of the family and solicited the help of U. S. Senator Lyndon B. Johnson. The senator arranged for Felix Longoria to be buried at the Arlington National Cemetery in Washington, D.C.

As well as being involved in civil rights issues, Dr. Hector P. García became involved in politics. He worked as a delegate and ambassador under Presidents Kennedy and Johnson. In 1965 the President of Panama, Marcos Robles, recognized Dr. García's services to humanity and awarded him the Order of Vasco Nuñez de Balboa.

Significantly, in 1984 Hector P. García was awarded by President Ronald Reagan the highest United States civilian honor, the Medal of Freedom! He is concerned with issues affecting Hispanics, such as the English-only movement and the spread of AIDS. Dr. Hector B. García is a civil rights activist and patriot. He is sometimes called the Martin Luther King, Jr. of Hispanics.

Suggested Activities

1. **Civil Rights Movement.** Hector P. García is often called the "Martin Luther King, Jr." of Hispanics. Read about Martin Luther King, Jr., and his work in the civil rights movement that not only helped African Americans but all oppressed people.

2. **Conflict Resolution.** When you have a problem, how do you solve it? Who are some people that you can turn to when you need help? Find out about conflict resolution. Conflict resolution is a popular program in schools across the country in which students help each other solve their own conflicts, using mediation techniques. Perhaps your own school has a similar program.

    Ask students to brainstorm a list of conflict situations that may occur among friends, in a school setting, or at home (perhaps among siblings). Divide the class into discussion groups. Have each group decide on a situation they would like to see resolved. Ask them to make a chart by dividing a piece of paper in half. Write the conflict situation at the top of the paper. Label one column "Reasons for Conflict" and the other "Possible Solutions to Problem." Ask group members to discuss and write their ideas on their charts. When all groups are done, have each group share their conflict situation and resolution with the class.

3. **Friendship Circle.** Have a friendship circle. All students sit in a circle. Have a fuzzy ball or something that students can hold onto while they are talking. Students take turns making a positive statement about the person sitting to their right; then they pass the warm fuzzy on to the next person who then shares. Only the person holding the fuzzy may speak. Prepare students ahead of time by asking them to think about what they appreciate about each other.

    Encourage students to use a variety of responses.

Recommended Reading _____

The People's Multicultural Almanac: America from the 1400's to the Present by The People's Publishing Group

Kids Explore America's Hispanic Heritage by Westridge Young Writers Workshop (John Muir Publications, 1992)

Great Lives: Human Rights by William Jay Jacobs (Macmillan, 1990)

People Who Make a Difference by Brent Ashabranner (SLJ, 1989)

Abbreviations

Dr. Hector P. García established the G. I. Forum, an organization designed to protect the civil rights of Mexican Americans, especially veterans. G. I. is an abbreviation for general issue, or government issue, usually pertaining to an enlisted person.

Listed below are several other abbreviations with which you may or may not be familiar. Try to write what each stands for next to the abbreviation. If you do not know one, use the dictionary or encyclopedia.

F. B. I. _____

C. I. A. _____

I. Q. _____

R. S. V. P. _____

V. I. P. _____

S. O. S. _____

N. A. S. A. _____

C. B. S. _____

U. S. M. C. _____

A. D. A. _____

A. B. C. _____

N. F. L. _____

U. F. W. _____

U. F. O. _____

Vilma Martinez

Civil Rights Attorney

Vilma Martinez is a well-respected attorney and public speaker who is known for her work in civil rights. Since she was a little girl, Vilma Martinez knew that she wanted to work for the rights of others. She did not like the way she sometimes saw her parents treated just because they were Mexican Americans. Her mother helped her to channel her energies when she was upset over prejudicial treatment. In high school, her counselors tried to dissuade her from going to college. They told her that she should go to a vocational school.

However, Vilma Martinez followed her own heart and went to college at the University of Texas in Austin where she earned her degree. After a professor's encouragement, she applied to and attended law school at Columbia University in New York City.

After law school, Vilma Martinez worked for the National Association for the Advancement of Colored People (NAACP) and was involved in some memorable cases. She later joined the prestigious law firm of Cahill, Gordon, and Reindel. During that time, Vilma Martinez was one of the first women to join the board of the Mexican American Legal Defense and Education Fund (MALDEF). By 1973, at the young age of twenty-nine, Martinez was president.

In MALDEF, Martinez accomplished many things, including the handling of cases concerned with voting rights for Mexican Americans as well as bilingual education issues. Most importantly, she made MALDEF a financially stable institution. She wanted MALDEF to be a strong organization that could continue to support the cause of Mexican Americans long after she was gone. In 1982, when she did leave MALDEF, it had become a national organization with a multimillion membership.

Upon leaving MALDEF, Vilma Martinez became a partner at the Los Angeles law firm of Munger, Tolles & Olson. She is often called upon to speak in public because of her wealth of experience in civil rights cases. She has lectured at several law schools, and she has been asked to serve as a board member for several organizations. She received the Jefferson Award for public service in 1976, and she won medals of excellence in 1978 and 1992 from Columbia University.

Suggested Activities

1. **Listening.** As a lawyer, Vilma Martinez must think critically and use all her senses of observation, listening for details. Attentive listening is often more difficult than it seems. Do the following listening activity with students in pairs.

Follow these guidelines:

- One person will be the listener and the other the speaker.
- The speaker has two minutes to speak uninterrupted on a topic or question the teacher will give.
- The listener must only listen and not speak at all.
- At the end of two minutes, the listener has one minute to tell or play back like a tape recorder what the speaker has said.
- The speaker then has an additional 30 seconds to make changes to the listener's response.
- Reverse roles and allow the speaker to become the listener.
- After the activity, discuss what it was like to play the different roles. Was it more difficult to be the listener or the speaker? Why?

---

2. **Twin.** Have students work in pairs. Ask them to pretend that they have an imaginary twin who does everything they do and is like them in every way. Have students describe to their partners what their twins are like. They should ask their partners to write down five positive statements about their twins. Have students reverse roles.

3. **Pair Drawing.** The following activity promotes cooperation. Give pairs of students one crayon or marker. The students will decide what they would like to draw. When the teacher says *begin*, the students both hold the one marker or crayon together and may not speak as they draw. Give the students about two minutes for the actual quiet drawing. Discuss how it felt to do the activity.

Recommended Reading _____

Girls and Young Women Leading the Way: 20 True Stories of Leadership by Frances A. Karnes and Suzanne M. Bean (Free Spirit Publishing, 1993)

Famous Mexican Americans by Janet Morey and Wendy Dunn (Dutton, 1989)

Women Who Changed Things by Linda Peary and Ursula Smith (Macmillan, 1983)

Personal Call to Action

Choose a current issue of concern to you and think about why it is significant. Think about what you would do to change things concerning this issue if you had the power to do so. Write an essay using your most persuasive language to convince others that your ideas for a solution are possible. Give your essay a title.

Suggested topics: Environmental Issues/ Homelessness/ Childcare and Recreational Facilities for Children/ Crime/ Poverty

_____

(Title)

by_____

_____

_____

_____

_____

_____

_____

_____

_____

_____

Edward R. Roybal

Congressman

Edward R. Roybal's mother instilled in him self-respect and perseverance. When he was young his mother bought him a suit and tie to wear to church on Sundays. He even wore a tie when he had an after-school job in high school. He was teased a lot by other children for wearing his tie, but he was preparing himself for his future. His parents always talked to him about going to college, and he never thought that he would not go to college.

However, in junior high school his counselors would not let him enroll in college preparatory classes because he was Mexican American. They put him in wood shop and industrial arts classes instead. When he told his mother what had happened, she talked to the principal, and Edward was soon put in classes he needed for college preparation. Edward Roybal was born in 1910 in Albuquerque, New Mexico. His father worked for the railroad, and after a strike by railroad workers failed, the family packed up and moved to East Los Angeles.

After completing high school, Roybal joined the Civilian Conservation Corps. It was the time of the Great Depression, and Roybal felt happy to have the opportunity to work in the Corps. In the Corps he helped build roads and fight forest fires. He gave most of his salary to his parents to help the family survive during the hard times. He quit working for the Corps to go to college at the University of California, Los Angeles. His first job after college was working for 20th Century Fox Studios. As a result of his job at the studio, he became involved in health education.

The Tuberculosis (TB) Association was visiting businesses, encouraging employees to take TB tests. Roybal began volunteering with the TB Association and eventually became the Health Education Director. In his job he increased public awareness about the dangers of TB, and he was also instrumental in getting the information to the Spanish speaking public. At the age of thirty-three, Roybal was elected to the Los Angeles City Council where he served for three additional terms.

In 1962 he was elected to the United States House of Representatives where he has been reelected time and time again. He did not abandon his concerns with health and education when he became a congressman. He was instrumental in the establishment of ten gerontology (the study of aging) clinics nationwide. He has also been in the forefront of those working on a national health plan. Edward Roybal is married and has three children. One of his daughters followed in her father's footsteps in politics by representing a district of Los Angeles in the California Assembly.

Suggested Activities

1. **Tuberculosis.** Edward R. Roybal became part of the Tuberculosis Association. Find out more about this disease. Who is more likely to attract this disease? What does the disease damage? How can you avoid attracting this disease?

2. **Racial Discrimination.** Edward R. Roybal was discriminated against in junior high school when his counselors would not let him enroll in college preparatory classes because he was Mexican American. How would you feel if you were Edward? Have you ever been discriminated against? Have you ever witnessed someone else being discriminated against? How would you react if you saw discrimination happening? What would you do to stop it? Why do you think some people feel superior to others?

3. **Noble Deed.** Edward R. Roybal has worked his entire life to help other people. Read the following tale to the students. When you have finished, discuss the questions that follow the story.

> There is a Mexican tale, "The Noblest Deed," that tells a story of a father of three sons who is about to die. The father has only one thing left to give his sons, a precious diamond. This diamond can not be sold or divided, and so he tells his sons that whoever does the most noble deed in one week will receive the diamond. After one week all three sons come back with their stories. The first had given half of what he owned to the poor of the city. The second had jumped into a river and pulled out a little girl caught in the swift current, even though he could hardly swim himself. The third had saved his bitter enemy from falling off a cliff, and they had become friends.

Questions:

• Which do you think was the noblest deed? Why?

• The father gave the diamond to the third son because he said a truly noble deed is one in which you risk your life for the sake of an enemy. Do you agree with his decision? Why or why not?

Recommended Reading

Tales the People Tell in Mexico by Grant Lyons (Julian Messner, 1972)

Mexican Folk Tales Retold, introduced by Juliet Piggott (Crane, Russak & Company Inc., 1973)

Hispanic Voters: A Voice in American Politics by Judith Harlan (Watts, 1988)

Bandera Personal

Make Your Own Personal Flag

Use the pattern below to create your own personal flag.

Section 1: On the left side, draw a picture and choose a color that describes a wish that you have for yourself.

Section 2: In the middle, write your name and draw a picture or tell something that you want to do or be when you are an adult.

Section 3: On the right side, draw a picture and choose a color that describes something that you do well.

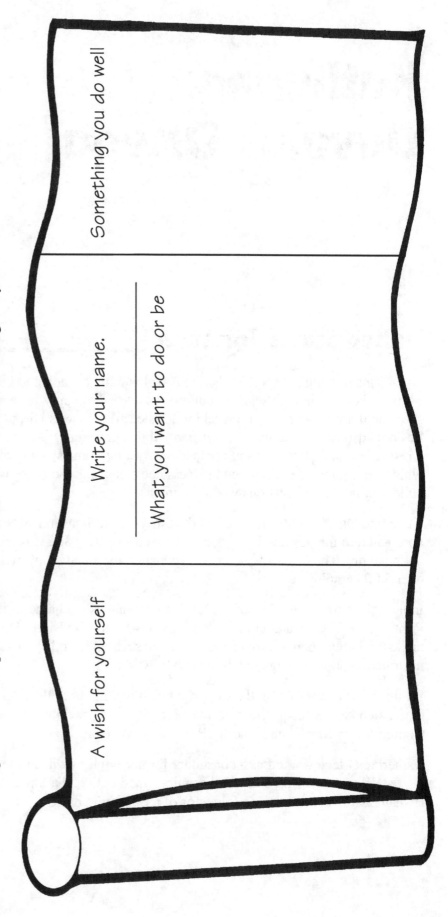

Something you do well

Write your name.

What you want to do or be

A wish for yourself

Katherine Davalos Ortega

United States Treasurer _____

Upon finishing high school, Katherine Davalos Ortega wanted to be a teacher. She wanted to teach business courses in high schools, but when she tried to apply for a teaching certificate she was told that she would not be able to get a teaching job because she was Hispanic. At that point, Ortega pursued a business career and started as a certified public accountant. As she was growing up, her family owned a restaurant, and all the children helped out. At that time she worked as a waitress and cashier. The whole family met and discussed business decisions, and the Ortegas' father always reminded his children that their educations would be their strengths.

Katherine Davalos Ortega served as the thirty-eighth treasurer of the United States after being nominated to the position by President Ronald Reagan. She was the second Hispanic woman to hold the position. The U. S. Treasurer is responsible for a budget of over $340 million and a large staff of over 5,000 employees.

In her job as treasurer, Katherine Davalos Ortega was in charge of the Bureau of Engraving and Printing, the U. S. Mint, and the U. S. Savings Bonds Division. During her tenure as treasurer, Ortega made the public more aware of the advantages and availability of savings bonds. She also made the information about savings bonds available in Spanish.

While she was working on the Copyright Tribunal in 1983, President Reagan recognized her talents and nominated her for the position of treasurer. She had previously been appointed to the Advisory Committee on Small and Minority Business Ownership.

Katherine Ortega worked as a consultant for her family-owned Ortero Savings and Loan in the late 1970s. When she worked at the Hispanic-owned Santa Ana State Bank in 1975, she became the first Hispanic woman president and director of a California bank.

Suggested Activities

1. **Discrimination.** When Katherine Davalos Ortega wanted to be a teacher, she was discouraged by those who said that she could not get a teaching job because she was Hispanic.

> Present the following scenario to the students.
>
> Imagine that you are standing in front of your class while a teacher, or someone else you respect, tells your classmates that you are inferior, not smart, and will not amount to much.

Ask students to respond to these questions:

- How would you feel?
- What would you do? What would you say to your classmates?
- What would you say to the teacher?
- What would you say to your family?

2. **Affirmation Tree.** Cover a container such as a coffee can with colored construction paper on which you have written "Affirmation Tree." Find a tree branch large enough to hold several cards tied to its twigs. Spray the branch with spray paint. Fill the container with plaster of Paris or sand and place the branch in the container. Divide the class into cooperative groups of four to six students. Have each group come up with an affirmation which they will write on an index card or rectangular piece of construction paper. Punch a hole in the top of each card and tie the cards onto the tree with yarn or cord.

Suggestions for affirmations include: "Don't Give Up!" "I Am Super," "I Am Smart," "I Am Sensational!," "Dream BIG!" etc.

3. **Take a Future Look.** Imagine yourself 10 to 15 years from now. You are in college, or you are working in your career field. What do you look like? What is your life like? Use markers, crayons, paints, and magazine pictures to make a collage representing how you see yourself in the future.

Recommended Reading _____

Women and Numbers by Teri Perl (Wide World Publishing, 1993)

Sometimes I Hate School by Carol Barkin and Elizabeth James (Raintree, 1975)

Working for Equality by Fiona MacDonald (Hampstead, 1988)

Friend Finder

Read the statements below. Find another person who can answer a question in one of the squares. Ask the person to explain the answer to you and have the person sign his or her name in the square. Each person may sign only one square on your paper. Keep finding friends to answer your questions until all the squares are full.

Find a friend who...

does not own a television.	has an abuela.	lives in a house where no one smokes.	has had his/her name mispronounced.
_____	_____	_____	_____
can explain who Cesar Chavez is.	is an artist.	can name three Mexican foods.	has a birthday the same month as yours.
_____	_____	_____	_____
is from a mixed heritage background.	has traveled out of the state.	can whistle.	knows what a migrant worker is.
_____	_____	_____	_____
can name three Spanish-speaking countries.	has pets at home.	has an amigo.	does not like pizza.
_____	_____	_____	_____

Dolores Huerta

Social Activist

Dolores Huerta, labor leader and social activist, has dedicated her life to the struggle for human rights and justice for farm workers. She is sometimes called Dolores "Huelga," which means "strike" in Spanish. She was born Dolores Fernandez on April 10, 1930, in the town of Dawson, New Mexico. Her parents divorced when she was young, and her mother moved with her three children to Stockton, California. Dolores' mother had high expectations for her children, and she encouraged Dolores to become involved in Girl Scouts and other clubs and activities.

As a young child, Dolores Huerta lived in an integrated neighborhood that was ethnically mixed. It was not until Dolores was a teenager that she experienced discrimination. Dolores attended Stockton College. Her college education was briefly interrupted by a marriage, the birth of two children, and subsequent divorce. She returned to college and got her A. A. degree. She worked at several jobs and eventually got her teaching certificate.

In the 1950s in Stockton, Dolores met Fred Ross. He was establishing the Community Service Organization (CSO) with the idea of organizing Mexican Americans. Although skeptical at first, Dolores soon joined CSO and worked on registering voters and, later, lobbying the state legislature in Sacramento, California. It was during this time that Dolores married her second husband, Ventura Huerta. In 1962, Dolores Huerta left the CSO to join Cesar Chavez in his effort to form the National Farm Workers Association (NFWA), later called the United Farm Workers Union (UFW).

In her work with the UFW, Huerta helped organize farm workers and lobbied and educated legislators about the poor living conditions of farm workers. For Huerta, her work has involved boycotting, striking, negotiating, and lobbying. Her marriage to Ventura Huerta also ended in divorce over tensions about Dolores' career, childcare, and domestic affairs.

In 1985, Dolores Huerta testified before the House of Representatives in their subcommittee hearings. Her duties include lobbying, policy making, and public appearances. She married Richard Chavez, Cesar's brother. Dolores Huerta has eleven children, all of whom were involved with the union at one time or another. They have all chosen various careers and are all proud of the work their mother has done to improve the lives of others.

Suggested Activities

1. **On the Road.** Dolores Huerta had eleven children. Often Dolores would take her children on the road with her as she tried to bring about change. How would you feel if your mother travelled a lot and took you along? Would you support your mother? What would you do if you did not want to go? Why do you think Dolores took her children with her?

2. **United Farm Workers.** Ask students to imagine that they are working for the United Farm Workers to help improve the poor living conditions of the farm workers. Each worker has been assigned the job of making posters that will draw attention to this needed change. Reproduce the activity on page 101. Have students make posters that will address this concern. Hang the signs in your classroom.

3. **Mexican Holidays.** Assign groups of students to find out more about the Mexican holidays listed below. Ask each group to make a presentation to the class. They should include information about the historical background and meaning of the holiday and how it is celebrated today. Students may wish to prepare foods and crafts for some of the holidays.

> January 6— *Día de los Reyes Magos* (Day of the Three Kings)
>
> February 24— *Mexican Flag Day*
>
> May 5— *Cinco de Mayo* (The fifth of May)
>
> May 10— *Día de la Madre* (Mother's Day)
>
> September 16— *Mexican Independence Day*
>
> October 12— *Día de la Raza* (Columbus Day)
>
> November 2— *Día de los Muertos* (Day of the Dead)
>
> December 12— *El Día de la Virgen de Guadalupe* (Our Lady of Guadalupe)
>
> December 16-25— *Las Posadas*
>
> December 24— *La Noche Buena* (Christmas Eve)
>
> December 25— *La Navidad* (Christmas Day)

Recommended Reading

Girls and Young Women Leading the Way: 20 True Stories of Leadership by Frances A. Karnes and Suzanne M. Bean (Free Spirit Publishing, 1993)

Fighting Fair: Dr. Martin Luther King, Jr., for Kids by Fran Schmidt and Alice Friedman (Grace Contrino Peace Foundation, 1990)

I Rigoberta Menchu: An Indian Woman in Guatemala by Rigoberta Menchu (Verso, 1984)

Create a Poster

Imagine that you are working to improve the poor living conditions of farm workers. You want to inform others of the problems facing the workers. Use the box below to create a poster that reflects your concerns and serves to inform the public.

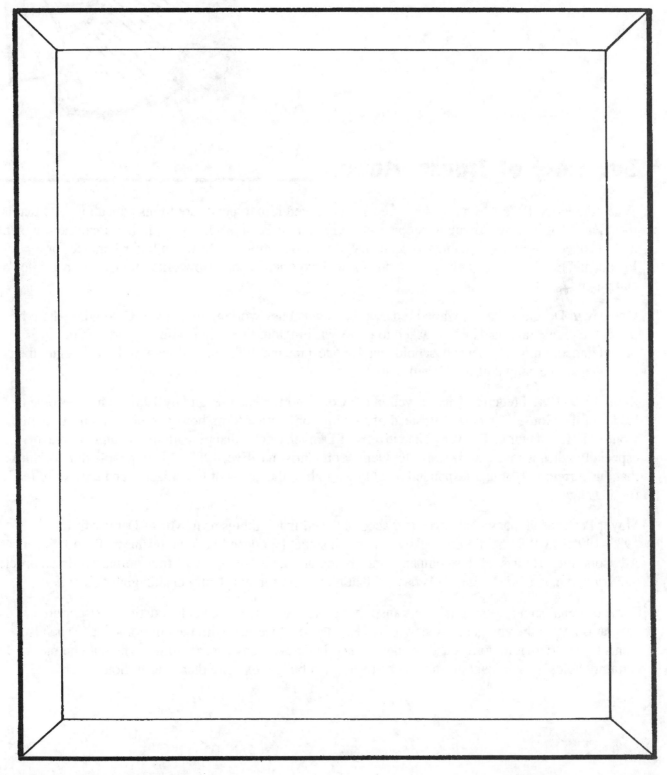

Frederico Peña

Secretary of Transportation

When Frederico Peña was a boy, his parents encouraged him to persevere in his education, and that is the advice that he gives to young people today. Frederico Peña is a husband, father, marathon runner, and President Clinton's appointee as secretary of transportation. Peña was a logical choice for President Clinton because Peña had much political experience and also worked tirelessly on Clinton's campaign.

One day in December 1992, while Frederico Peña was busy working in Denver, Colorado, where he lived, the phone rang and he was asked to go to Washington, D. C. His wife supported him by organizing and moving their household, and by late January, 1993, he and his family had begun their new lives in the capital of the United States.

From 1979–1982 Frederico Peña served in the Colorado Legislature, and by 1981 he had become the leader of the House Democrats. Instead of running for another term, however, he announced that he would run for mayor of Denver. The citizens of Denver were unhappy with the incumbent mayor, especially when a severe snowstorm hit Denver on Christmas Eve, 1982. Many people did not think that the current mayor had responded quickly enough to the needs of the citizens, and they were ready for a change.

Mayor Peña faced many challenges and accomplished many things as mayor of Denver from 1983–1991. In 1991 he did not seek reelection; instead, he opened his own business, Peña Investment Advisors, Inc. He has left his company since being appointed secretary of transportation. In an article in _Hispanic_ magazine, Frederico Peña said that he believes in constantly challenging yourself.

Some of Peña's plans as secretary of transportation are to increase funds to existing transportation programs and to thereby generate new jobs. He is also concerned with the environment. Peña also wants to ensure that minority- and women-owned businesses have access to government contracts. He certainly holds a significant position as he oversees a budget of more than four billion dollars.

Suggested Activities

1. **Clean Air Conservation.** In his job as secretary of transportation, Frederico Peña supports existing mass transportation programs because of his concern for the environment. Have a large group discussion on smog and cars. How many students have parents who have had smog inspections on their cars? Why is this important?

2. **Air and Water Pollution.** Air and water pollution are causing environmental hazards all over the world. Study the effect the 900-mile Amazonia Highway is having in Brazil. Study the effects of the destruction of the rain forest and animal habitats. Discuss and study the role of water pollution on plants and animals in the forest.

3. **Earth Day.** Study Earth Day and its purpose. Organize an Earth Day celebration at your school. Contact the National Wildlife Federation or the National Arbor Day Foundation for resources.

4. **Aerosol Products.** Ask students to survey the number of aerosol cans in their homes. Talk about the importance of using nonaerosol products.

5. **Concept Map.** Have students create a concept map of environmental issues. Each time an issue is raised, think of other related issues. Use the example below to create a concept map.

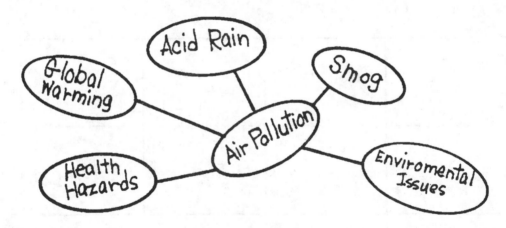

As a class, create an "Issues Awareness" chart of the "number one environmental issues," as seen by members of the class. The chart could include the following categories: the topic (air pollution, water pollution, etc.); a statement of the problem and how it was created; a list of community, state, or government agencies or groups trying to solve the problem; and students' suggestions on how to solve the problem. Encourage students to research the environmental issues and to write letters to appropriate agencies. Have students report back to class on the information they have gathered.

Recommended Reading

This Is the Way We Go to School by Edith Baer (Scholastic, Inc., 1990)

Fiesta by Beatriz Zapater and José Ortega (S & S Trade, 1993)

50 Simple Things Kids Can Do to Save the Earth by The Earth Works Group (Greenleaf Pubs. 1990)

Transportation Graphs

1. Survey your classmates to find out how they come to school. Use the bar graph below to depict your results. If you were to survey the teachers at your school, do you think the results would be different? How? Why?

2. Are there any students who gave you two or more answers to your question about how they get to school? Do some students sometimes walk and sometimes ride their bikes? Make a Venn diagram to depict these findings.

3. Brainstorm all the possible modes of transportation that you can think of. Survey your classmates to see who has used the various modes of transportation. Make a graph to show your findings; use pictures cut out of magazines to illustrate. Are there any modes of transportation that no one in your class has ever used? For example, has anyone in your class ridden in a blimp? in an airplane? on a motorcycle?.

4. Are there any modes of transportation that you can think of that are no longer used today? Write a paragraph describing what it would be like to travel in a covered wagon, for example. What modes of transportation that we use today will be outdated in the future? Why do you think so? Invent a new mode of transportation for the 21st century. Write a paragraph describing it and draw a picture of your new invention.

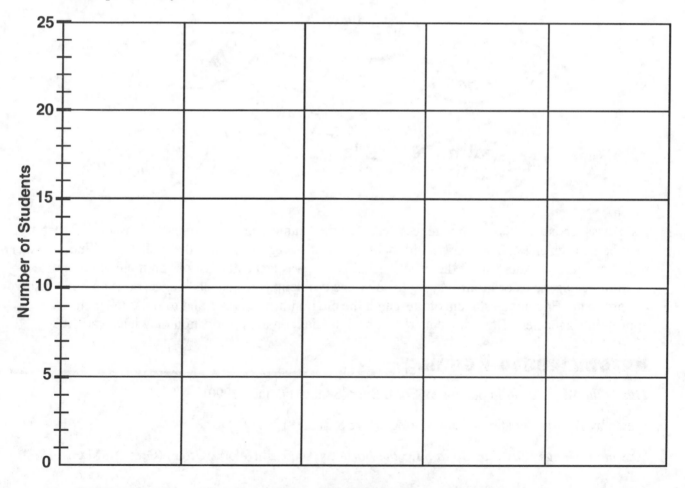

Method of Transportation

Collaboration for Change

Cesar Chavez and Dolores Huerta, along with the United Farm Workers, worked to change things for the better. In small groups of four to six students, work together to identify and to take steps to change a situation or problem at your school (graffiti in the restrooms or school bullies, for example).

Use the following questions as guides.

1. As a group, brainstorm some possible problems to address.

2. Poll other students at your school to see whether they identify the same problems that your group did or whether they can think of other ideas.

3. Narrow down your ideas to one choice. With which problem will you deal?

4. How long has this problem existed at the school? How many people does it affect?

5. What are some possible solutions? Brainstorm within your group and poll other students in the school.

6. What plan of action does your group intend to take?

7. Does your plan of action require the support or cooperation of others? How?

8. What are some possible consequences, both negative and positive, of your solution?

9. How will you know whether your solution has been successful?

10. Share the results of your actions with your classmates.

11. What would you do differently if you had to do it again?

Leadership Qualities

Many of the leaders featured in this section are famous because they have gone beyond what is required in their jobs and have tried to improve the quality of life for others. Many of the leaders have won awards and prizes for their dedication to the community. Pretend that you are a famous leader and are about to receive a prize for something you have done. At the awards presentation, someone will be speaking of your accomplishment and describing what kind of person you are. On the lines below, write the speech that the person will give as he/she presents you with your award. Do not forget to include your name, the accomplishment for which the prize is being awarded, and a glowing description of your best qualities.

Name _____

Accomplishment _____

Who Are They?

For each of the sections in this book, have students reflect on the Hispanic Americans highlighted and their contributions in the areas of Education and Scholarship, Fine Arts, Science and Medicine, Sports, and Civic Leadership.

Have students write responses to the section questions on page 108. This may be done as each section is completed, or it can be used as an end-of-the-book activity. (Note: You may wish to reproduce the page, cut along the dashed lines, and distribute each section as needed.)

Ask students to use a separate piece of paper for each section's responses. When the questions are completed, continue with the remainder of the activities on this page.

1. Ask students to lay out their pages in front of them and review what they wrote and drew. Does any one of the occupations appeal to them more than another? Why?

2. Discuss the pages one by one, using the following questions to promote reflection.

- Is the portrait male or female?

- Is the description positive or negative?

- Do the students' works share common elements? (Do many of their scientists' portraits wear glasses, for example?)

- Did the students draw or describe people who are like themselves in any way? Why or why not?

- Did the students list people they knew in each category? Why or why not?

---

3. Direct the discussion to talk about the notion that artists, teachers, scientists, athletes, and leaders are just ordinary people like you and me. Also, they can be male or female, young and old, Black, Asian, Anglo, or Hispanic.

4. At the end of the discussion, ask the students to share whether they gained any insights after looking at their classmates' work or whether any of their ideas had changed as a result of discussion.

5. Try repeating this activity in a few months, choosing different occupations. See how the students respond similarly or differently from now.

Who Are They? *(cont.)*

Who Is a Teacher?

Think about teachers. What does a teacher look like? What does a teacher do? What kind of person is a teacher?

On a piece of paper, write a description of a teacher. Explain what you think exemplifies the qualities a teacher should have. Below your responses, draw a portrait of a teacher.

Who Is an Artist?

What do you think about when you hear the word "artist?" What does an artist look like? What kind of a person do you think an artist is?

On a piece of paper, write a description of what you think an artist is. Below your description, draw a portrait of an artist. At the bottom of the paper, write the names of some artists you know.

Who Is a Scientist?

Think about scientists. What comes to mind when you hear the word "scientist?" What does a scientist do? What kind of a person do you think a scientist is? What special talents or qualities do you think a scientist needs to be successful at his or her job?

On a piece of paper, write a description of a scientist. Below your description, draw a portrait of a scientist. If you know any scientists, write their names at the bottom of the paper.

Who Is an Athlete?

Think about athletes. What does an athlete look like? What does an athlete do? What physical and intellectual abilities do you think an athlete needs to succeed?

On a piece of paper, write a description of what you think an athlete is. Below your description, draw a picture of an athlete. At the bottom of your paper, write the names of athletes you know.

Who Is a Leader?

What do you think about when you hear the word "leader?" What kind of person is a leader? What does a leader do? What special abilities do you think a leader must have to succeed?

On a piece of paper, write a description of what you believe a leader is. Below your description, draw a portrait of a leader. At the bottom of your paper, list some leaders you know.

Mexican Tree of Life

The Tree of Life is an elaborate, candle-bearing sculpture, usually created out of clay. Because it is meant to depict the creation of nature, the tree is decorated with flowers, birds, animals, people, and fruit. Each Tree of Life is different, varying by height, size, intricacies, and number of candle holders (anywhere from one to perhaps a dozen). The Tree of Life originated with the Moors and was brought to Spain in the eighth century. Eventually it was introduced into Mexico. The potters of Izucar de Matamoros in Puebla and the Metepec region of Mexico are famous for this elaborate art form.

Make your own Tree of Life. When you have completed it, place it on a large paper plate that you have decorated with pictures or words that represent what you have learned about the Hispanic Americans presented in this book.

Materials: short glass beverage bottle, three small paper clips, paintbrush, self-hardening clay, assorted clay tools, tempera or acrylic paint, two paper plates

Directions:

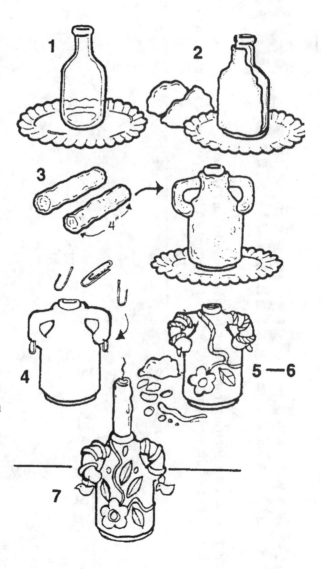

1. Place the bottle on top of a paper plate. The plate will help you rotate the sculpture, and it will also serve as a work area.

2. Cover the bottle with the clay. Do not put clay on the bottom of the bottle or cover the top opening.

3. Roll out two pieces of clay to form fat, sausage shapes about 4" (10 cm) long. Attach these shapes as illustrated, one on each side of the bottle near the neck. These are the branches of the tree.

4. Break one paper clip in half to make two hooks. Insert the straight end into each branch. The curved hook end must be sticking out. This will be used to support hanging clay bird ornaments.

5. With the remaining clay, sculpt and attach large leaves and flower shapes to the tree. Make two birds and insert a paper clip into the top of each body.

6. When the clay sculpture hardens, paint it with vibrant colors. Hang the birds from the hooks on the branches.

7. Remove the Tree of Life from the used paper plate. Insert a short candle into the neck of the bottle.

Hispanic Americans—Who Are They?

This map shows the countries from which the families of many Hispanic Americans came. Work in small groups to research traditions and basic facts of one of the countries. Present your information in a report to be shared with the class.

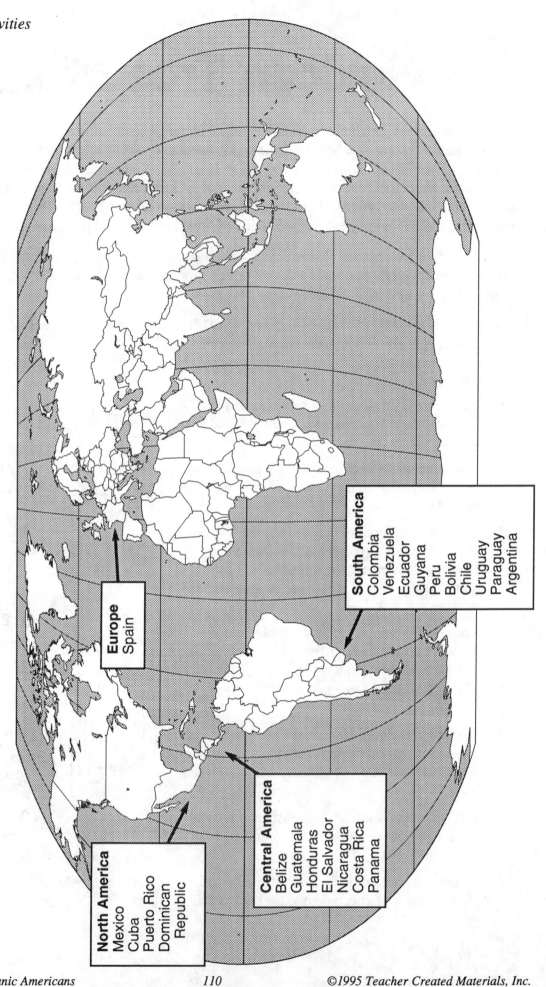

Europe
Spain

South America
Colombia
Venezuela
Ecuador
Guyana
Peru
Bolivia
Chile
Uruguay
Paraguay
Argentina

North America
Mexico
Cuba
Puerto Rico
Dominican
Republic

Central America
Belize
Guatemala
Honduras
El Salvador
Nicaragua
Costa Rica
Panama

Answer Key

Page 20

Los Angeles — city of angels

Colorado — colored red

San Francisco — Saint Francis

Montana — mountain

San Antonio — Saint Anthony

Los Cruces — the crossroads

Texas — tile roof (Spanish meaning for a Native American name.)

Santa Fe — Holy Faith

El Paso — the passage

San Diego — Saint James

Page 81

1. 1966
2. 1967
3. 1968
4. the second
5. 1960 and 1962
6. 1964
7. 76
8. .351
9. 138
10. 1962 and 1965

Page 89

F. B. I. - Federal Bureau of Investigation

C. I. A. - Central Intelligence Agency

I. Q. - Intelligence Quotient

R. S. V. P. - Respondez s'il vous plait (French for please reply)

V. I. P. - Very Important Person

S. O. S. - Save Our Ship

N. A. S. A. - National Aeronautics and Space Administration

C. B. S. - Columbia Broadcasting System

U. S. M. C. - United States Marine Corps

A. D. A. - American Dental Association

A. B. C. - American Broadcasting Company

N. F. L. - National Football League

U. F. W. - United Farm Workers

U. F. O. - Unidentified Flying Object

Bibliography

Burciaga, Antonio José. *Undocumented Love: Amor Indocumentado.* (Chusma House Publications, 1992)

Drotar, David L. *Fun Science Learn and Discover Book.* (Playmore Inc., 1984)

Duvall, Lynn. *Respecting Our Differences: A Guide to Getting Along in a Changing World* (Free Spirit Publishing, 1994)

Foster, David Williams. *A Dictionary of Contemporary Latin American Authors.* (Center for Latin American Studies: Arizona State University, 1975)

Fraden, Dennis Brindell. *Remarkable Children.* (Little Brown & Co., 1987)

Garza, Hedda. *Joan Baez.* (Chelsea House Publishers, 1991)

Hawxhurst, Joan C. *Antonia Novello.* (The Millbrook Press, 1993)

Holt, Marion and Julianne Dueber. *1001 Pitfalls in Spanish,* 2nd ed. (Barron's Educational Series, Inc., 1986)

Meier, Matt S. *Mexican American Biographies: A Historical Dictionary 1836–1987.* (New York: Greenwood Press, 1988)

Morey, Janet and Wendy Dunn. *Famous Mexican Americans.* (New York: Cobblehill Books, 1989)

Newlon, Clark. *Famous Puerto Ricans.* (New York: Dodd Mead & Co., 1975)

Perez, Dr. Theresa. *Portraits of Mexican Americans: Pathfinders in Mexican-American Communities.* (Good Apple, 1991)

Stefoff, Rebecca. *Gloria Estefan.* (Chelsea House Apple, 1991)

Telgen, Díane and Jim Kamp. Eds. *Notable Hispanic Women.* (Gale Research Inc, 1993)

Wohl, Gary and Carmen Cadilla Ruibal. *Hispanic Personalities: Celebrities of the Spanish-Speaking World.* (Regents Publishing Company, 1978)

Recommended Reading for Teachers:

Comprehensive Multicultural Education by Christine Bennett (Allyn Bacon, 1990)

Beyond Language by Bilingual Education Office (California State Department of Education, 1986)

Minority Education by Tove Skutnabb Kangas and Jim Cummins (Multilingual Matters, 1988)

With Different Eyes edited by Faye Peitzman and George Gadda (California Academic Partnership Program, 1991)

Crossing the Schoolhouse Border by Laurie Olsen, Project Director (California Tomorrow, 1988)